THEY DID THEIR WORK BRAVELY

Civil War Generals
Buried in Pennsylvania

David L. Callihan

HERITAGE BOOKS
2004

HERITAGE BOOKS
AN IMPRINT OF HERITAGE BOOKS, INC.

Books, CDs, and more – Worldwide

For our listing of thousands of titles see our website
at
www.HeritageBooks.com

Published 2004 by
HERITAGE BOOKS, INC.
Publishing Division
65 East Main Street
Westminster, Maryland 21157-5026

International Standard Book Number: 0-7884-2501-3

To My Wife Jean

Whose Support and Encouragement

Made This Book Possible

TABLE OF CONTENTS

PHILADELPHIA: Laurel Hill Cemetery

PHILADELPHIA: Philadelphia National Cemetery

PHILADELPHIA: St. Dominic's Churchyard

PHILADELPHIA: St. James The Less Churchyard

YORK: Prospect Hill Cemetery

ALPHABETICAL LISTING OF THE GENERALS

INTRODUCTION

I have been a Civil War enthusiast for about as long as I can remember. In 1987 my wife and I toured West Point, and one of the places we visited was the Post Cemetery there. In particular, we were interested in seeing the grave of George Armstrong Custer. As we were walking through the cemetery, searching for Custer's grave, I saw the graves of many Civil War generals, whose names were quite familiar to me – Buford, Sykes, Scott, Kilpatrick, Keyes, etc. I took photos of these graves and some others (including Custer's), and when I got home I looked in Ezra Warner's *Generals in Blue* and discovered that over 20 Civil War generals are buried at West Point. I was living in Harrisburg, Pennsylvania, at that time, and I saw that two generals were buried in Harrisburg Cemetery. I visited that cemetery and I photographed both of their graves. By now I was hooked, and ever since I have been pursuing my hobby of finding and photographing the graves of the Civil War generals, both Union and Confederate. So far my ongoing quest to find and photograph all of their graves has taken me to 41 states, Canada, and Washington, D.C., and I have found the grave sites of 995 of the 1008 full rank generals. Along the way I have learned (initially to my great surprise) that I was not alone in pursuing this hobby. I have met and corresponded with numerous fellow grave hunters, sharing photos, directions to cemeteries, and other information. And now I am the editor/publisher of *Grave Matters* (www.gravematters.net), which is a newsletter about Civil War grave sites.

In the past ten years or so, guide books have been published concerning the grave sites of Civil War generals buried in Georgia, Tennessee, Mississippi, Louisiana, Michigan, and Texas, and in 1997 a book was published concerning the grave sites of all 425 full rank Confederate generals. No such book has been published concerning the generals' grave sites in Pennsylvania. There are 45 full rank generals buried in the Keystone State (including one Confederate general), ranging from Philadelphia to Pittsburgh, and several towns and cities in between.

The book is arranged by the cities or towns where the generals are buried. A biographical sketch is provided for each general, so that the reader and grave site visitor can obtain a better understanding of these generals and their war records. One or more photos are provided for each grave site, as well as a map of the cemetery or directions for finding each grave site. Only one of these 45 grave sites is unmarked (Baker in Huntingdon Valley), and most of the grave markers at the other 44 grave sites are in reasonably good shape. It is my hope that readers of this book will visit some if not all of these grave sites, and thereby honor the countless thousands who struggled in that war for their ideals and principles. It's a fascinating journey.

David L. Callihan
December 2004

PENNSYLVANIA

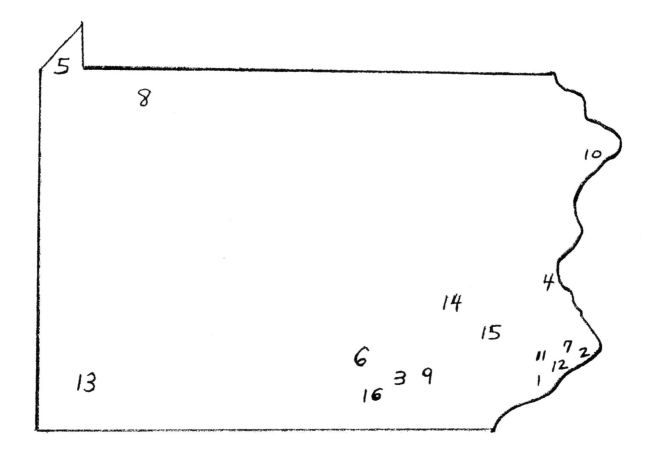

1. Bala Cynwyd	5. Erie	9. Lancaster	13. Pittsburgh
2. Bristol	6. Harrisburg	10. Milford	14. Pottsville
3. Columbia	7. Huntingdon Valley	11. Norristown	15. Reading
4. Easton	8. Kane	12. Philadelphia	16. York

BALA CYNWYD

WEST LAUREL HILL CEMETERY

HERMAN HAUPT

Born: March 26, 1817
Died: December 14, 1905

General Haupt was born in Philadelphia and he graduated from West Point in 1835 at the age of 18, ranked 31st out of 56. Three months later he resigned his commission and embarked on a career in engineering. Prior to the Civil War his employment involved civil and railroad engineering, teaching math and engineering at Pennsylvania College in Gettysburg, writing treatises on bridge construction, and working as a superintendent of a railroad company.[1]

In the summer of 1861 Haupt applied for the newly created position of Assistant Secretary of War, but he did not receive the appointment. In April 1862 Secretary of War Edwin Stanton appointed Haupt chief of construction and transportation for the U.S. Military Railroads, with the grade of colonel. Stanton gave Haupt wide powers to seize and operate all railroads, and make use of any equipment necessary, to improve the efficiency of the military railroads. For the next 17 months Haupt wielded that power and brought order and efficiency to the railroad system. On September 5, 1862, he was appointed brigadier general of volunteers, although he had indicated that he would be willing to perform his military services without rank or pay, so that he could continue with his private business ventures. He continued his invaluable services for the military until September 14, 1863, when he chose to officially decline his commission and resign from military service, rather than submit to the restrictions required by the military.[2]

For the next 42 years Haupt continued to lead a successful and diverse life. He published more treatises, he worked as a railroad engineer, manager, and president, and he was involved in pipeline and pneumatic drill development. Ironically, after spending so many years working with railroads, he died of a heart attack aboard a train in Jersey City, New Jersey. It is interesting to note that civil engineer is listed first on his grave marker, rather than his military grade of brigadier general. This likely reflects Haupt's attitude as to which of those two occupations had been more significant.[3]

HERMAN HAUPT
CIVIL ENGINEER
BORN PHILA
MARCH 26 1817
DIED
DEC. 14 1905
BRIG. GENERAL
U.S.A.

West Laurel Hill Cemetery is located at 215 Belmont Avenue, just off of City Avenue (US Route 1), near the Philadelphia County line. Upon entering the cemetery, follow the signs to the cemetery office. As shown on the map, when you stand in the office parking area with your back to the office, the road leading to Haupt's grave is in front of you. Haupt's grave is in the Norriton Section, next to the road in the cemetery, as marked on the map.

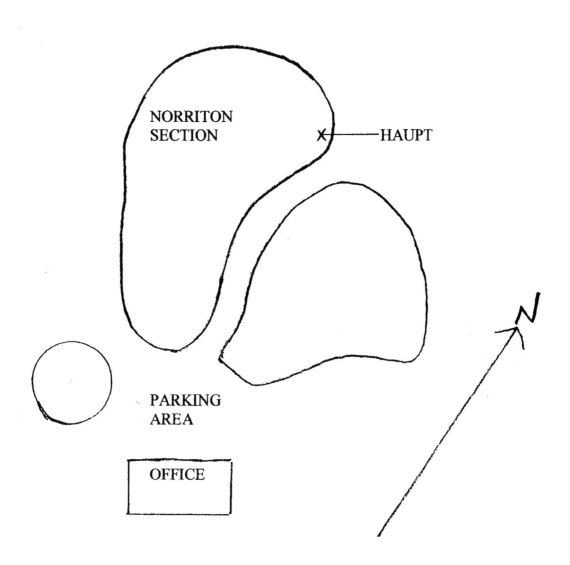

BRISTOL

ST. JAMES EPISCOPAL CHURCHYARD

WILLIAM READING MONTGOMERY

Born: July 10, 1801
Died: May 31, 1871

General Montgomery was born in Monmouth County, New Jersey, and he graduated from West Point in 1825, ranked 28th in a class of 37. He served on the frontier, on the Canadian border, in Florida during the Second Seminole War, and then in Texas on garrison duty before the Mexican War. During the latter war, while serving as a captain in the 8th Infantry, he was wounded at both Resaca de la Palma and Molino del Rey and he was brevetted to major and lieutenant colonel for gallantry. In December 1852 he was promoted to major. Three years later he was stationed at Fort Riley, Kansas. Pro-slavery forces in Kansas that opposed Montgomery succeeded in having him dismissed in December 1855 on allegations of appropriating a portion of military lands at the fort for the creation of a town.[1]

In May 1861 Montgomery organized the 1st New Jersey Volunteers and he was named colonel of the regiment on May 21, 1861. Although his regiment was in General Irvin McDowell's reserves at First Manassas and saw no action in that battle, in August 1861 Montgomery was commissioned brigadier general of volunteers to date from May 17, 1861. He spent the rest of the war far away from the battlefields, mainly serving in administrative posts, such as military governor of Alexandria, Virginia, commander of

Union forces at Annapolis and later at Philadelphia, and military commissioner in Memphis.[2]

Health problems forced Montgomery to resign from the army on April 4, 1864. He dealt in wood molding in Philadelphia for a while and then he spent the remainder of his life at his home in Bristol, Pennsylvania, where he died.[3]

The St. James Episcopal Churchyard is located at the corner of Walnut and Cedar Streets in downtown Bristol, which is northeast of Philadelphia. Montgomery's grave is near Cedar Street, in the back corner of the churchyard.

COLUMBIA

MOUNT BETHEL CEMETERY

THOMAS WELSH

Born: May 5, 1824
Died: August 14, 1863

General Welsh was born and raised in Columbia, Pennsylvania.[1] He was engaged in the lumber business in Columbia prior to the Mexican War. He saw considerable action in that war, serving in the armies of both Zachary Taylor and Winfield Scott. During the war he rose from a private in the 2nd Kentucky to a second lieutenant in the 11th U.S. Infantry, and at the Battle of Buena Vista he was severely wounded. Upon his return to Columbia after his discharge in 1848, he was successful as a merchant, a canal boat owner, a justice of the peace, and a lock superintendent.[2]

In April 1861 Welsh was involved in the recruitment of the 2nd Pennsylvania, a ninety-day regiment, and he was named lieutenant colonel of the regiment on April 20. The regiment was mustered out in July 1861, and in October 1861 he became colonel of the 45th Pennsylvania. After briefly serving as a brigade commander at Charleston Harbor from April to July 1862, he commanded a brigade in the 9th Corps at South Mountain and Antietam. Welsh was named brigadier general of volunteers on November 29, 1862, but the Senate failed to act on his appointment, and so on March 13, 1863, he was reappointed. In April 1863 he reported for duty in Cincinnati and he was given command of a division in the 9th Corps. Welsh's division was one of two 9th Corps divisions sent to Mississippi in June to support the Union effort against Vicksburg. In early August, with that campaign successfully completed, the division was loaded on boats and sent back north to Ohio. Welsh became ill with a fever and chills (possibly malaria) soon after the boat left Snyder's Bluff, Mississippi. When his boat arrived at Cairo, Illinois, Welsh was too ill to proceed farther on a common railroad car. A sleeping car was found and he was transported to Cincinnati. He arrived in that city on August 14, 1863, but he died there later that same day.[3]

Mount Bethel Cemetery is located on Locust Street, between 7th and 8th Streets, in downtown Columbia. When you enter the cemetery you will immediately come to a circle. Go halfway around this circle, taking the road off from the circle that is basically opposite the road you entered on. Continue on this road until you come to a T intersection. Welsh's grave will be in front of you, slightly to your left.

BRIG. GEN. THOMAS WELSH
BORN IN COLUMBIA PA.
MAY 5, 1824.
DIED IN CINCINNATI OHIO
AUGUST 14, 1863.

EASTON

EASTON CEMETERY

CHARLES ADAM HECKMAN

Born: December 3, 1822
Died: January 14, 1896

General Heckman was born in Easton, Pennsylvania, and at the age of 15 he graduated from the Minerva Seminary in Easton. He worked as a hardware store clerk prior to the Mexican War. During that war he served as a sergeant in the Regiment of Voltigeurs and Foot Riflemen. After the war he resided in Phillipsburg, New Jersey, where he worked as a railroad conductor for the New Jersey Central Railroad.[1]

Heckman was commissioned lieutenant colonel of the 9th New Jersey on October 8, 1861. He was promoted to colonel on February 10, 1862, and he led his regiment in the early phases of General Ambrose Burnside's North Carolina Expedition. He was wounded on March 14, 1862, at New Bern. From April 2 until July 6, 1862, he commanded a brigade in Burnside's force. On July 26 he was wounded at Young's Cross Roads. Heckman was commissioned brigadier general of volunteers to rank from November 29, 1862. Between December 1862 and April 1864 Heckman served in the Carolinas and southeastern Virginia, at various times commanding several different brigades and divisions, and the Union forces at New Bern, Beaufort, and Newport News.[2]

On April 28, 1864, Heckman was given command of a brigade in the 18th Corps in the Army of the James, and he was wounded at Port Walthall, Virginia, on May 7. Nine days later, during the Battle of Drewry's Bluff, his brigade was routed and Heckman was captured. Heckman was imprisoned at Charleston, South Carolina, where he was one of 51 captive Union officers placed within range of the Union artillery, in an attempt to stop the Union bombardment of that city. In September 1864 he was exchanged and immediately placed in command of a division in the 18th Corps. During the September 29 attack against Fort Harrison near Richmond, Heckman took over command of the corps when its commander, General Edward O.C. Ord, was wounded. Later Ord was quite critical of Heckman's handling of this assault.[3]

In January and February of 1865, Heckman commanded the 25th Corps in the absence of its commander, General Godfrey Weitzel, but this was his last service in the field. On March 23, 1865, General Ulysses S. Grant relieved Heckman of duty, based on a belief that he was not fit for field command. Heckman returned home and he resigned on May 25, 1865. Subsequently Heckman worked as a public utility contractor and a train dispatcher for the New Jersey Central Railroad. He died at his son's home in Germantown, Pennsylvania.[4]

Easton Cemetery is located at 401 N. 7th Avenue in Easton. There are section markers on the trees in the cemetery. Heckman's grave is in Section D, in the back left of the cemetery.

ERIE

ERIE CEMETERY

STRONG VINCENT

Born: June 17, 1837
Died: July 7, 1863

General Vincent was born in Waterford, Pennsylvania. After attending Erie Academy and Trinity College, Vincent graduated from Harvard University in 1859. He studied law and opened his own law office in Erie, but the start of the war cut short his law career. Quickly volunteering after the firing on Fort Sumter, on April 14 Vincent enlisted in the Wayne Guards, a three-month Pennsylvania militia regiment. He was named first lieutenant and adjutant of the regiment on April 21. The regiment was sent to Pittsburgh, where it remained until it was mustered out on July 25. Then he helped raise the 83rd Pennsylvania and was commissioned the regiment's lieutenant colonel on September 14, 1861.[1]

The regiment was assigned to the 5th Corps in the Army of the Potomac, and it participated in the Peninsula Campaign in the spring of 1862. On May 27, 1862, the regiment saw its first action at Hanover Court House, Virginia. Several weeks later Vincent became ill with a fever (possibly malaria or typhoid fever). From his hospital bed he heard the sounds of fighting at Gaines Mill on June 27, and he insisted on joining his regiment the next day at Savage Station. Vincent took command of the regiment, but he was soon overcome with his illness and he was carried from the field unconscious. He was sent back home, where he slowly recovered, and he did not rejoin his regiment until October 1862. In the meantime the absent Vincent had been promoted to colonel of the

10

regiment on June 27, 1862, due to the death of the regiment's colonel. He gallantly led his regiment in one of the futile charges against Marye's Heights at Fredericksburg on December 13, 1862. At Chancellorsville the regiment saw little action, but in the reorganization after that defeat, Vincent became the commander of a brigade in the 5th Corps on May 20, 1863.[2]

At Gettysburg the largely untested Vincent proved worthy of his promotion. During the Confederate assault of July 2 against the Union left, Vincent's brigade was behind the front lines, awaiting orders to advance. A messenger rode up to Vincent with orders for Vincent's division commander. Vincent insisted that the courier read the message to him. Learning that troops were desperately needed at Little Round Top, Vincent violated military protocol and assumed responsibility for moving his brigade to the undefended height without direct orders from a superior officer. His troops arrived on Little Round Top and assumed a defensive position on the south slope of the hill approximately five minutes before General Evander Law's Alabamians attacked the height. At one point in the ensuing fight Vincent was mortally wounded while trying to rally his men as they were being pushed back. He died on July 7, unaware of the fact that he had been commissioned brigadier general of volunteers on July 3.[3]

Erie Cemetery is located at 2116 Chestnut Street, between 19th and 26th Streets. Vincent's grave is in the middle of Section 1.

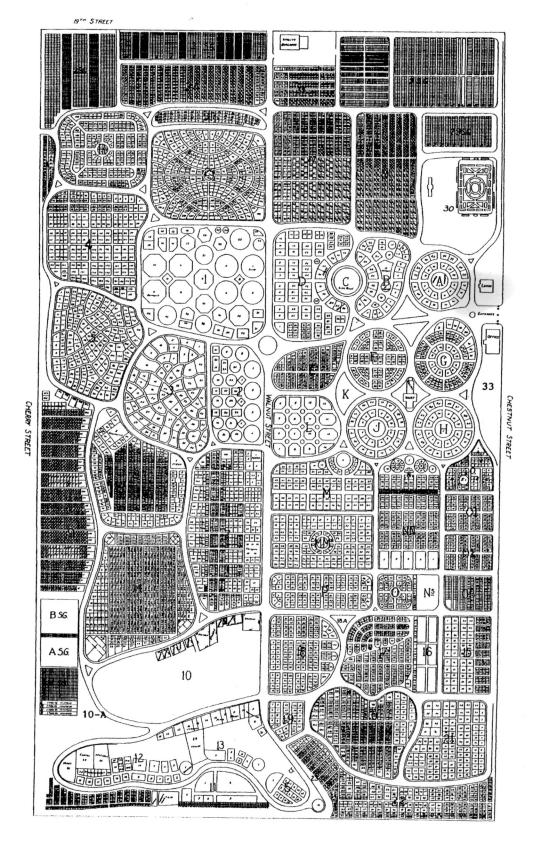

HARRISBURG

HARRISBURG CEMETERY

JOHN WHITE GEARY

Born: December 30, 1819
Died: February 8, 1873

General Geary was born in Mount Pleasant, in western Pennsylvania. His education at Jefferson College was cut short upon the death of his father. In order to support his family he pursued several different careers, such as schoolteacher, store clerk, lawyer, and surveyor. Also, he had been active in local militias. In the Mexican War, while serving as lieutenant colonel of the 2nd Pennsylvania Infantry, he was wounded five times at Chapultepec. He later became the regiment's colonel. After the war he lived in California, where he organized postal services and served as the first mayor, or alcalde, of San Francisco. In 1856 Geary was named territorial governor of Kansas, where he supported the anti-slavery forces. After his resignation from that post in March 1857 he lived on his farm in Pennsylvania.[1]

Geary raised and organized the 28th Pennsylvania Infantry and in June 1861 he became its colonel. The regiment was assigned to General Nathaniel Banks' forces at Harpers Ferry. Geary was wounded in the leg during a skirmish in October 1861 and he was promoted to brigadier general of volunteers on April 25, 1862. Commanding a brigade at Cedar Mountain in August 1862, Geary was seriously wounded in the ankle and arm, but he returned to duty two months later. He led a division of the 12th Corps at Chancellorsville and Gettysburg. In the former battle he was struck in the chest by a cannonball, but he suffered no serious injuries, other than an inability to speak for several weeks. Thus Geary was wounded a total of nine times in his military career, which was

13

remarkable even considering the fact that he was an easy target, being six feet, six inches tall.[2]

Geary continued to ably command his division during the Chattanooga Campaign, and upon the consolidation of the 11th and 12th Corps, he commanded the 2nd Division of the 20th Corps in 1864-1865 in the Atlanta Campaign, during the March to the Sea, and in the Carolinas. While serving as military governor of Savannah in January 1865 he received a brevet promotion to major general of volunteers.[3]

Although he had always been a Democrat, Geary was twice elected governor of Pennsylvania as a Republican war hero, serving from January 1867 to January 1873. Shortly after leaving office he died in Harrisburg.[4]

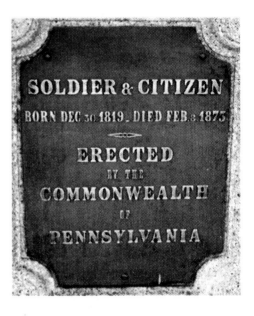

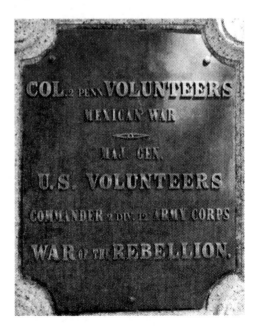

HARRISBURG

HARRISBURG CEMETERY

JOSEPH FARMER KNIPE

Born: March 30, 1823
Died: August 18, 1901

General Knipe was born in Mount Joy, Pennsylvania, and he received a minimal education in several area schools. After practicing the trade of shoemaker in Philadelphia, Knipe entered the U.S. Army in 1842 as a private. He saw action in the Dorr Rebellion in Rhode Island and in the Mexican War. After his discharge from the army in 1848 he worked for the Pennsylvania Railroad in Harrisburg.[1]

Early in the Civil War Knipe served as a brigade inspector of militia in Pennsylvania. In October 1861 he became colonel of the 46th Pennsylvania, which served under General Nathaniel Banks in the Shenandoah Campaign of 1862 and at Cedar Mountain. Knipe was wounded in the right shoulder and knee at Winchester on May 25, 1862. Then on August 9 at Cedar Mountain he was wounded twice again, on the scalp and in the right hand, and he had to be carried from the field. He led a brigade of the 12th Corps during the Antietam Campaign. On April 15, 1863, he was commissioned brigadier general of volunteers to rank from November 29, 1862. During the Gettysburg Campaign Knipe led Pennsylvania militia organized to face the Southern invaders.[2]

Knipe served as a brigade and division commander in the 12th and 20th Corps during the Chattanooga and Atlanta Campaigns. At the battle of Resaca on May 15, 1864, he was slightly wounded in the left shoulder. Later Knipe was sent to Memphis to recruit and organize cavalry deserters. He performed well as a cavalry division commander during the Battle of Nashville in December 1864.[3]

Knipe was mustered out in August 1865, and from 1866 until 1869 he served as postmaster of Harrisburg. This was the first of several state and Federal positions held by Knipe after the war, most notably superintendent of the federal penitentiary at Fort Leavenworth, Kansas. Knipe died in Harrisburg. His badly weathered original grave marker was recently replaced with an exact duplicate.[4]

Harrisburg Cemetery is located at the end of 13th Street, just off of State Street, near downtown Harrisburg. As marked on the map, Geary's grave is in Section M at the western edge of the cemetery and Knipe's grave is in Section R near the road in the cemetery. President Lincoln's first Secretary of War, Simon Cameron, is buried in Section U.

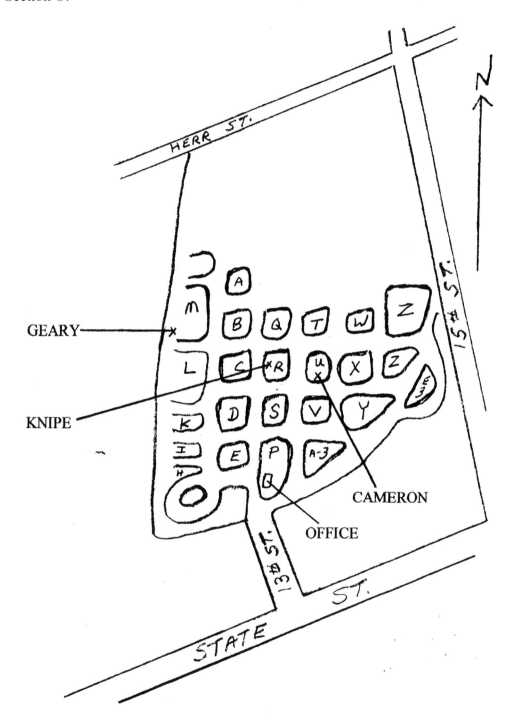

HUNTINGDON VALLEY

FOREST HILLS CEMETERY

LaFAYETTE CURRY BAKER

Born: October 13, 1826
Died: July 3, 1868

General Baker was born in Stafford, New York and he grew up in Michigan. Little is known about his formative years. Shortly before the start of the Civil War, Baker was in California, where he was a member of the Vigilance Committee of San Francisco. This law and order organization provided him with useful experience for his later espionage activities.[1]

With the start of the war Baker returned to the East. He soon was employed as a spy for the North, but he was captured while attempting to acquire intelligence on the Rebel encampment at Manassas, Virginia. Baker convinced his captors of his Southern sympathies and he was permitted to return to the North as an agent for the South. Instead Baker provided the Federal government with information on the Confederate position and plans.[2]

Next Baker was appointed a special agent by Secretary of War Edwin Stanton to run an espionage network from Washington. Suspected Southern spies and sympathizers were arrested and harassed. Later, when the Pinkerton Detective Agency fell into some disfavor, Baker was made the head of the National Detectives, a secret police force operating under Stanton. In this capacity Baker was involved in a variety of activities, such as investigating bounty jumpers, counterfeiters, and corrupt government contractors.[3]

Immediately after President Abraham Lincoln's assassination, Stanton had Baker arrange the pursuit of John Wilkes Booth and David Herold, which resulted in Booth's death and Herold's capture. Baker had been named a colonel of the 1st District of Columbia Cavalry on May 5, 1863, and now he was commissioned a brigadier general of volunteers to date from April 26, 1865, the date of Booth's death and Herold's capture.[4]

With the end of the war, Baker's power and influence quickly diminished. President Andrew Johnson dismissed Baker as a result of allegations that Baker had abused his powers and lined his pockets with kickbacks during his espionage activities. Nothing was proven and no formal charges were ever filed against Baker. During the impeachment trial of Johnson, Baker was again involved in controversy, when he alleged he possessed damaging letters against the President, but he could not produce them.[5]

Baker died in Philadelphia and was buried in the Mutual Family Cemetery. At a later date all of the graves in that cemetery were moved en masse to Forest Hills Cemetery with no records of precise burial locations being maintained. It is assumed Baker's remains are in an open field at Forest Hills, in an unmarked grave, where literally thousands of others removed from various area cemeteries are likewise buried in unmarked graves. The only marker in that open field is an old obelisk for a family named Ronaldson.[6]

Forest Hills Cemetery is located at Byberry Road and Philmont Avenue in Huntingdon Valley, just outside of the Philadelphia city limits. It is very near the place where Philadelphia, Bucks, and Montgomery Counties meet. Baker's unmarked gravesite is likely to be in the open area around the Ronaldson marker, which is in the far northeast area of the cemetery.

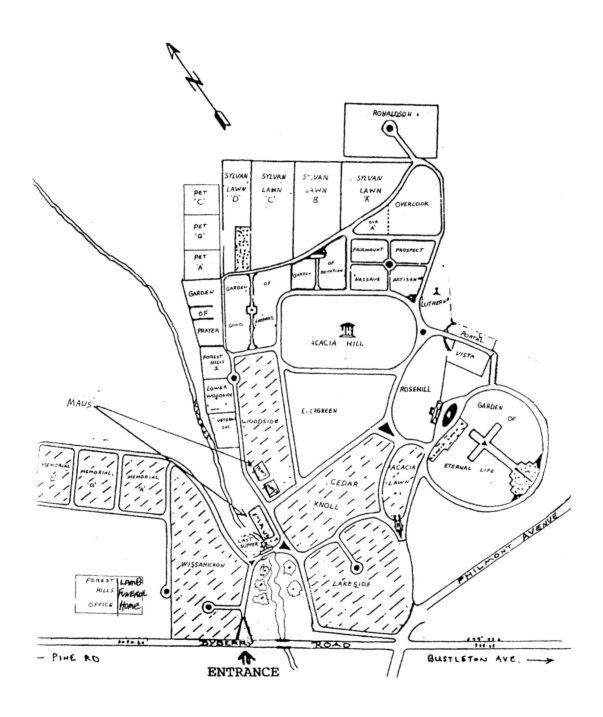

KANE

KANE CHAPEL

THOMAS LEIPER KANE

Born: January 27, 1822
Died: December 26, 1883

General Kane was born in Philadelphia and he received an extensive education in both the United States and overseas, including Paris. Kane studied law under his father and he became a U.S. Commissioner. He was an ardent abolitionist and so he refused to enforce the Fugitive Slave Law. Kane resigned his post, and his father, the District Judge, had him jailed for contempt. The U.S. Supreme Court overruled this action, and upon his release from jail, Kane worked as an agent in the Underground Railroad, assisting runaway slaves in finding freedom in the North.[1]

Kane became a friend and associate of Brigham Young and the Mormons during their migration west to Utah, and in 1858 he helped defuse the friction between the Mormons and the U.S. government. Kane soon returned to Pennsylvania and he founded the town of Kane in northwestern Pennsylvania. When the Civil War began, he recruited men from that rural area to form the 13th Pennsylvania Reserves, or Bucktails as they were called, because of the buck's tail they wore on their hats.[2]

Commissioned lieutenant colonel of the regiment in June 1861, Kane saw his first action at Dranesville, Virginia on December 20, 1861. During this fight he was wounded in the right cheek, resulting in the loss of several teeth and permanent impaired vision. Then on June 6, 1862, at Harrisonburg, Virginia, he was seriously wounded in the right knee and captured. A Confederate soldier broke Kane's breastbone when he struck Kane with the butt end of a rifle. In August 1862 Kane was exchanged for Lieutenant Colonel Williams C. Wickham, who, like Kane, would later become a general.[3]

On September 7, 1862, Kane was promoted to brigadier general of volunteers. He was given command of a brigade in the 12th Corps on October 6, 1862, although at first he was unable to ride a horse and he had to walk with crutches as a result of his earlier leg wound. During the Chancellorsville Campaign he contracted pleurisy and pneumonia. It is reported that while recuperating in a hospital in Baltimore (or Philadelphia) he learned of the likelihood of a battle in Pennsylvania, and so he left his sickbed and arrived at Gettysburg in time to rejoin his brigade on July 2. Even though this story probably exaggerated the truth, it is known that he arrived at Gettysburg on July 2 and he led his brigade in its fight to retake Culp's Hill on the morning of July 3. But this would be his last field command in the war, for by November 1863 Kane was compelled to resign from the army because of complications from his wounds and other health problems. In 1865 he received a brevet promotion to major general of volunteers for his performance during the Gettysburg Campaign.[4]

Kane spent the remainder of his life residing in both Kane and Philadelphia, and he pursued careers as an author, president of the state board of charities, and a railroad president. He died in Philadelphia and was originally buried in the Kane family vault at Laurel Hill Cemetery in Philadelphia (see photo below). The vault is located in Section P, on the edge of a steep cliff overlooking the Schuylkill River. In November 1884 his remains were removed and reburied beside the Kane Chapel in Kane, Pennsylvania, which is maintained by the Mormons. His association with the Mormons was such that a statue of Kane (identical to one at the Kane Chapel) is today displayed inside the State Capitol Building in Salt Lake City, Utah.[5]

The Kane Chapel is located at 30 Chestnut Street in the small town of Kane, which is in the northwest part of the state. Kane's grave is next to the chapel.

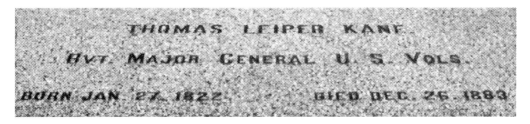

LANCASTER

LANCASTER CEMETERY

JOHN FULTON REYNOLDS

Born: September 20, 1820
Died: July 1, 1863

General Reynolds was born in Lancaster, Pennsylvania.[1] In 1841 he graduated from West Point, ranked 26th out of 52. He served on garrison duty at various posts along the Atlantic and on the frontier. During the Mexican War he earned brevet promotions to captain and major, and after the war he continued the routine life of garrison duty. In September 1860 he returned to West Point to serve both as the Commandant of Cadets and as an instructor of tactics.[2]

On May 14, 1861, Reynolds was named lieutenant colonel of the 14th U.S. Infantry and on August 20, 1861, he was commissioned brigadier general of volunteers. He commanded a brigade of the Pennsylvania Reserves in the defenses of Washington, D.C. during the winter of 1861-1862 and he briefly served as military governor of Fredericksburg, Virginia. His brigade joined the Army of the Potomac on the Peninsula in June 1862. Early on the morning of June 28, 1862, after the Union retreat from the battlefield of Gaines Mill, Reynolds was captured. He was sent to Libby Prison in Richmond and in August 1862 he was exchanged for Brigadier General Lloyd Tilghman, who had been captured the previous February at Fort Henry, Tennessee.[3]

At Second Manassas Reynolds commanded a division and directed a delaying action at Henry Hill that enabled the defeated Union army to safely leave the field. During the Antietam Campaign he commanded Pennsylvania militia that had been mustered in anticipation of a Confederate invasion of the Keystone State. He was promoted to major general of volunteers on November 29, 1862, and he was in command of the 1st Corps at Fredericksburg and Chancellorsville. Tradition has it that after the latter battle President Abraham Lincoln offered Reynolds command of the Army of the Potomac, but the offer was declined because Lincoln was unable give Reynolds assurances that he would command the army without any interference from the politicians in Washington.[4]

In late June 1863 the new army commander, General George G. Meade, named Reynolds commander of the army's left wing, consisting of the 1st, 3rd, and 11th Corps, and he sent Reynolds' command forward into Pennsylvania to find the invading Rebel army and to bring it to battle. On the morning of July 1 the Battle of Gettysburg began when Confederate infantry attacked Federal cavalry west of the town. Later that morning Reynolds arrived in the town, just ahead of the lead elements of the 1st Corps. Shortly thereafter, while placing his infantry into position along McPherson Ridge, Reynolds was shot in the head and died instantly. He was greatly respected and his death was mourned by friend and foe alike.[5]

Lancaster Cemetery is located in downtown Lancaster. Go north on Lime Street (US Route 222 North). Then turn right on Lemon Street, which will lead you directly to the cemetery entrance. Immediately after entering the cemetery you will come to a circle. Reynolds' grave is near the circle, over to your left.

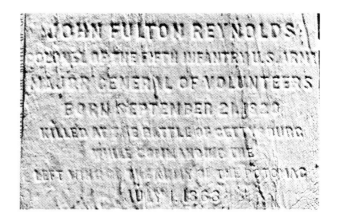

MILFORD

MILFORD CEMETERY

CHARLES HENRY VAN WYCK

Born: May 10, 1824
Died: October 24, 1895

General Van Wyck was born in Poughkeepsie, New York and he grew up in Bloomingburg, New York. After graduating first in his class at Rutgers in 1843, he became a lawyer and he served as district attorney of Sullivan County, New York from 1850 to 1856. Having switched from a Democrat to a Republican, Van Wyck was elected to Congress in 1858, and he served there until March 3, 1863.[1]

On September 4, 1861, Van Wyck was commissioned colonel of the 56th New York, a regiment he had recruited. Although his regiment saw little action during the Peninsula Campaign, Van Wyck received a minor wound in his left knee on May 31, 1862, at Fair Oaks. In December 1862 his regiment was transferred to the Charleston, South Carolina area, where it remained for the rest of the war. In January 1865 he was given command of a brigade in the Department of the South and in June 1865 he was temporarily assigned to command the Military District of Western South Carolina. On September 27, 1865, he was commissioned brigadier general of volunteers, thereby receiving one of the last four full rank commissions in the war.[2]

Politics dominated the rest of Van Wyck's life. He was a U.S. Representative from New York from March 1867 to March 1869, and from February 1870 to March 1871. He moved to Nebraska in 1874, was a member of the 1875 constitutional convention, served in the Nebraska state senate from 1876 to 1880, and was a U.S. Senator from Nebraska from 1881 to 1887. His political influence waned when he introduced a constitutional amendment to create the direct election of senators rather than by the vote of the state legislatures. The Nebraska Legislature did not reelect him to the U.S. Senate in 1886, and in subsequent elections he lost bids for governor and state senator. After spending the remainder of his life as a rancher, he died in Washington, D.C. He was buried in Milford, Pennsylvania, his wife's home town.[3]

Milford Cemetery is located on US Routes 206/209, south of town. Enter the cemetery, then bear right at the first fork in the road. At the next fork bear right again. After that, turn left at the second left, which is a gravel road. Van Wyck's grave will shortly be on your left, across from the Pinchot mausoleum.

NORRISTOWN

MONTGOMERY CEMETERY

WINFIELD SCOTT HANCOCK

Born: February 14, 1824
Died: February 9, 1886

General Hancock was born in the hamlet of Montgomery Square, near Norristown, Pennsylvania. He graduated from West Point at the age of 20 in 1844, ranked 18th out of 25. He served on the frontier for two years and then he served in the Mexican War. During that war he received a minor leg wound at Churubusco and he earned a brevet to first lieutenant for gallantry. After the war he again served on the frontier and he participated in the Utah Expedition against the Mormons. At the start of the Civil War he was a captain and the chief quartermaster in Los Angeles.[1]

Hancock was appointed brigadier general of volunteers on September 23, 1861. As a brigade and division commander on the Peninsula, during the Antietam Campaign, at Fredericksburg, and at Chancellorsville, he consistently won praise for his leadership. Minor wounds at both Fredericksburg and Chancellorsville did not force him to leave either battlefield. He was promoted to major general of volunteers to rank from November 29, 1862, and after Chancellorsville he became commander of the 2nd Corps.[2]

On July 1, 1863, his friend General George Meade chose Hancock to replace the fallen General John Reynolds as commander of the Union forces on the battlefield at Gettysburg. Hancock arrived on the field around 4 p.m., just in time to observe the 1st and 11th Corps retreating to the heights south of town. Hancock's calmness and military bearing helped bring order out of the chaos that afternoon, and quickly the Union forces rallied and dug in to present a bold front on Cemetery and Culp's Hills. With the death of

Reynolds, Hancock now became Meade's most dependable subordinate. On July 2 Meade gave Hancock expanded command of the army's left wing, and under Hancock's calm leadership the Union forces halted the ferocious Confederate assault against the Union left. On July 3 during the artillery bombardment that preceded Pickett's Charge, Hancock's presence near the front lines helped calm his troops at the center of the Union line. Unfortunately during the Rebel infantry assault Hancock suffered a serious groin wound which never properly healed. Gettysburg was the finest moment in his illustrious career.[3]

Hancock led his 2nd Corps throughout the Overland Campaign of 1864, but finally in November 1864 problems with his Gettysburg wound forced him to leave active field command. He then commanded the Veteran Reserve Corps in Washington. In August 1864 he was named brigadier general in the Regular Army and in 1866 he was promoted to major general in the Regular Army.[4]

After the war Hancock held various departmental commands. In 1880 he was the Democratic nominee for President, but he lost to James Garfield by a narrow margin. Hancock died at Governors Island, New York, in command of the Department of the East, a position he had held since November 1877. He was one of the finest field commanders in the war, and on many battlefields he earned his sobriquet, "Hancock The Superb."[5]

NORRISTOWN

MONTGOMERY CEMETERY

JOHN FREDERICK HARTRANFT

Born: December 16, 1830
Died: October 17, 1889

General Hartranft was born near Pottstown, Pennsylvania. He attended Marshall College and then he graduated from Union College in New York in 1853, after studying civil engineering. After working as a civil engineer, he studied law and was admitted to the bar in 1860.[1]

On April 20, 1861, Hartranft became colonel of the 4th Pennsylvania, which was mustered into U.S. service as a three-month regiment. In July the regiment advanced with General Irvin McDowell's army toward Manassas, Virginia, but on the eve of the first major battle in the war the regiment left the field, based on the fact that its ninety-day enlistment term had ended. Hartranft's pleas to his men to remain with the army and fight were ignored. Hartranft remained with McDowell's army, and during the Battle of First Manassas he worked as a volunteer aide-de-camp for General William Franklin. In August 1886 Hartranft was awarded a Medal of Honor for his actions at this battle.[2]

Hartranft next raised the 51st Pennsylvania and on November 16, 1861, he was appointed colonel of the regiment. The regiment served in General Ambrose Burnside's 9th Corps in North Carolina in the spring of 1862 and at Antietam in September 1862. During the latter battle the 51st was one of the first regiments to get across Burnside's Bridge. Hartranft exercised brigade and division command in the 9th Corps throughout 1863, although he was still a colonel. Finally his performance at Spotsylvania Courthouse in May 1864 earned him a commission as brigadier general of volunteers to date from May 12, 1864. His gallantry during the repulse of the Confederate assault against Fort Stedman, near Petersburg, Virginia, on March 25, 1865, resulted in a brevet promotion to major general of volunteers.[3]

Hartranft's next assignment was as special provost marshal for the Lincoln assassination conspiracy trial. After mustering out in 1866, Hartranft became involved in politics in Pennsylvania, holding such posts as governor, auditor general, postmaster of Philadelphia, collector of the port of Philadelphia, and commander of the Pennsylvania National Guard. He died in Norristown.[4]

NORRISTOWN

MONTGOMERY CEMETERY

ADAM JACOBY SLEMMER

Born: January 24, 1829
Died: October 7, 1868

General Slemmer was born in Montgomery County, Pennsylvania.[1] He graduated from West Point in 1850, ranked 12th out of 44. He served in Florida, he performed garrison duty in California for four years, and he taught several different subjects at West Point from 1855 to 1859.[2]

In January 1861 Slemmer was first lieutenant of artillery in command at Fort Barrancas near Pensacola, Florida. When Florida declared itself seceded from the Union on January 10, 1861, Slemmer moved his command to Fort Pickens across Pensacola Bay. Fort Pickens remained in Union hands throughout the war, because of Slemmer's quick decision. On May 14, 1861, he was named major of the 16th U.S. Infantry.[3]

In the autumn of 1861 Slemmer was the acting inspector general for the Department of Western Virginia, but in October he contracted typhoid fever and was so gravely ill that it was feared he would die. In May 1862 he was finally able to return to field command, leading the 16th U.S. Infantry in its campaigns that summer and autumn. On December 31, 1862, during the Battle of Stones River, Slemmer was seriously wounded in the left knee while leading his command. The next day Confederate cavalry captured him, but they quickly released him because he could not be removed from the field. He was in a hospital for two months and then on sick leave until July 1863, although upon his return to duty he could only walk with crutches. Consequently, his days of active campaigning were over, and he spent the rest of the war in Ohio, serving as the presiding officer of a board for examination of sick and wounded officers. In April 1863 he was commissioned brigadier general of volunteers to rank from November 29, 1862. In 1865 he was brevetted brigadier general in the Regular Army.[4]

Slemmer was mustered out on August 24, 1865, but he remained in the army, serving on garrison duty and as a member of a board for examination of candidates for promotion. He died while serving as commander of Fort Laramie, Dakota Territory (Wyoming).[5]

NORRISTOWN

MONTGOMERY CEMETERY

SAMUEL KOSCIUSZKO ZOOK

Born: March 27, 1821
Died: July 3, 1863

General Zook was born in Chester County, Pennsylvania.[1] He grew up at the home of his maternal grandparents on the campground of Valley Forge. He was active in the Pennsylvania militia, being named adjutant of the 100th Pennsylvania Militia when he was only nineteen. In 1842 he began to work for the Washington and New York Telegraph Company in Philadelphia, and, after he was promoted to superintendent in 1846, he worked in New York City. He then began to participate in the New York militia. Zook was also credited with making several important discoveries regarding electricity.[2]

At the start of the Civil War Zook was lieutenant colonel of the 6th New York Militia, and he and the regiment quickly reported for duty at Annapolis. He served as military governor of Annapolis at the time of the Battle of First Manassas. After the enlistment period for his regiment expired on July 31, 1861, Zook recruited the 57th New York and he was named colonel of the regiment on October 19, 1861. The regiment, led by Zook, was assigned to the 2nd Corps and it participated in the Peninsula Campaign. Zook was on medical leave during the Antietam Campaign.[3]

On October 6, 1862, Zook was given command of a brigade in the 2nd Corps. At Fredericksburg on December 13, 1862, he was wounded while gallantly leading his men in one of the many futile assaults against Marye's Heights and the sunken road. On March 23, 1863, he was commissioned brigadier general of volunteers effective November 29, 1862. Zook continued to command his brigade at Chancellorsville and

Gettysburg. On the afternoon of July 2, 1863, his brigade advanced into the Wheatfield at Gettysburg to reinforce General Daniel Sickles' 3rd Corps. During the advance Zook was wounded in the abdomen and he died the next day in a nearby field hospital. He was posthumously brevetted major general of volunteers.[4]

Montgomery Cemetery is located at the western end of downtown Norristown. From downtown Norristown, go west on Main Street. Turn left on Hartranft Avenue, which ends at the entrance to the cemetery. Hancock's grave is in the northeast corner of the cemetery, and Hartranft's grave is in the southeast corner. As marked on the map, Slemmer's grave is a short distance from the dirt road in the cemetery, and Zook's grave is near the road.

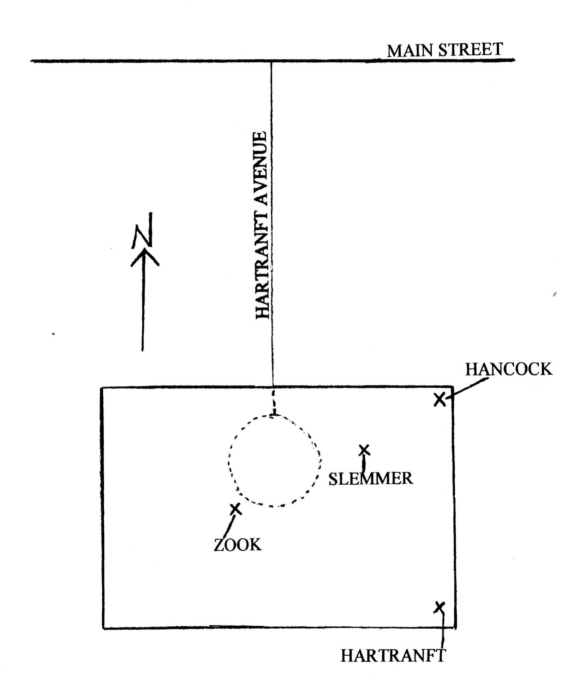

PHILADELPHIA

CHRIST CHURCH CEMETERY

GEORGE CADWALADER

Born: May 16, 1806
Died: February 3, 1879

General Cadwalader was born in Philadelphia to a prominent family.[1]   He practiced law in that city and he was very active in the local militia. In 1844 he was a brigadier general of the Pennsylvania militia and in that capacity he was instrumental in ending the anti-foreigner riots in Philadelphia that occurred as a result of the activities of the American or Know-Nothing political party. On March 3, 1847, he was commissioned brigadier general in the United States army and he ably commanded forces during the Mexican War. He was brevetted major general for his gallantry at Chapultepec.[2]

On April 19, 1861, Cadwalader was appointed major general of Pennsylvania militia and he commanded Union forces in Baltimore in May 1861 during a time of great turmoil in that city. In July 1861 he commanded a division in the Department of Pennsylvania. He received a commission as major general of volunteers on April 25, 1862.[3]

Although Cadwalader never commanded troops in combat during the Civil War, he served his country in a variety of capacities behind the lines. He served on several military boards and commissions, he commanded garrisons, he worked as an advisor to the President and Secretary of War, and he served as commander of Union forces in Philadelphia. On July 5, 1865, he resigned from the army and returned to his private interests. He served as the Commander in Chief of the Pennsylvania Commandery of the

Military Order of the Loyal Legion of the United States (MOLLUS) from its inception in 1865 until his death in Philadelphia in 1879.[4]

Christ Church Cemetery is located in downtown Philadelphia at the intersection of Arch and 5th Streets. If the cemetery is locked, you will have to make arrangements with the staff at Christ Church (located a few blocks away on 2nd Street) to have someone unlock the cemetery for you. Once you are inside the cemetery, look for the entrance gate at 5th Street. Both Cadwalader and McCall are buried near this entrance, next to the path that leads to that entrance.

PHILADELPHIA

CHRIST CHURCH CEMETERY

GEORGE ARCHIBALD McCALL

Born: March 16, 1802
Died: February 26, 1868

General McCall was born in Philadelphia and he graduated from West Point in 1822, ranked 26th out of 40. He spent the next twenty years on garrison duty, mainly in Florida. For five years (1831-1836) he was as an aide-de-camp to General Edmund P. Gaines and he served in the Second Seminole War in Florida. During the Mexican War he won brevets to major and lieutenant colonel for gallantry at Palo Alto and Resaca de la Palma. In 1850 he became a colonel and he was appointed inspector general of the army. He resigned in April 1853 because of health problems and he retired to his estate near West Chester, Pennsylvania.[1]

McCall came out of retirement with the start of the Civil War, and on May 15, 1861, he was appointed major general of Pennsylvania Volunteers. Only two days later he was commissioned brigadier general of volunteers in the federal service. McCall commanded the Pennsylvania Reserves, which was assigned to the defenses of Washington, D.C. during the winter of 1861-1862. In early June 1862 the Pennsylvania Reserves were sent to the Peninsula to join the Army of the Potomac in that army's campaign against Richmond. The Reserves were designated the third division of the 5th Corps, and they were heavily engaged in the early fighting of the Seven Days Campaign at Mechanicsville and Gaines Mill. By all accounts McCall performed well during this fighting. Then at Glendale on June 30, 1862, he was wounded and later captured when he accidentally rode into the Confederate lines while reconnoitering. After being held prisoner at Libby Prison in Richmond, he was exchanged on August 18, 1862, for General Simon B. Buckner, who had been captured in February 1862 at Fort Donelson.[2]

McCall saw no more active service in the war. Upon his exchange he was on sick leave until his resignation on March 31, 1863. He again retired to his farm where he died.[3]

(See directions for grave site on Page 38.)

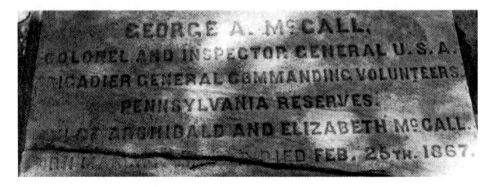

PHILADELPHIA

LAUREL HILL CEMETERY

WILLIAM HENRY CHARLES BOHLEN

Born: October 22, 1810
Died: August 22, 1862

General Bohlen was born in Bremen, Germany, but he moved to Philadelphia in his youth. He became wealthy as a liquor dealer and he served as a private in the Pennsylvania Volunteers during the Mexican War.[1]

Bohlen recruited the 75th Pennsylvania and became its colonel on September 30, 1861. The 75th was largely comprised of German immigrants living in Philadelphia. In December 1861 Bohlen was given command of a brigade in General Louis Blenker's division. Bohlen's brigade spent the winter of 1861-1862 stationed in the defenses of Washington, D.C. In late March 1862 Blenker's division was sent to the Mountain Department, which was commanded by General John C. Fremont. On April 28, 1862, Bohlen was commissioned brigadier general of volunteers. On June 8, 1862, at the end of the Valley Campaign of 1862, Fremont attacked General Thomas J. (Stonewall) Jackson's Confederate forces at Cross Keys, Virginia. Although the battle resulted in a Union defeat, Bohlen performed well as a brigade commander during this battle.[2]

In late June 1862 Bohlen was given command of a brigade in General Franz Sigel's 1st Corps of General John Pope's Army of Virginia. Bohlen capably covered the retreat of Union forces from the battlefield of Cedar Mountain on August 9, 1862. On August 22, 1862, Sigel directed Bohlen to send his brigade across the Rappahannock River at Freeman's Ford, in order to conduct a reconnaissance against the rearguard of

.

Stonewall Jackson's forces. After crossing the river, the Union forces observed a large Confederate wagon train that appeared to be unguarded. Bohlen was ordered to seize the seemingly vulnerable train. Almost immediately after the Federals began their advance toward the train, an unseen Confederate brigade attacked Bohlen's right flank. Then two more Confederate brigades arrived on the scene and joined in the attack on Bohlen's lone brigade. Soon Bohlen's brigade was routed and Bohlen was shot through the heart during his brigade's withdrawal across the river.[3]

PHILADELPHIA

LAUREL HILL CEMETERY

SAMUEL WYLIE CRAWFORD

Born: November 8, 1827
Died: November 3, 1892

General Crawford was born in Franklin County, Pennsylvania.[1] He graduated from the University of Pennsylvania in 1846 and from that university's medical school in 1850. In March 1851 he became an assistant surgeon for the army and for the next nine years he served in that capacity at a variety of posts in the West. In the winter of 1860-1861 he was stationed at Fort Moultrie and Fort Sumter at Charleston, South Carolina, as surgeon for those posts. He commanded a battery at Fort Sumter during the Southern bombardment of that fort in April 1861.[2]

On May 14, 1861, Crawford was named major of the 13th U.S. Infantry, and he was commissioned brigadier general of volunteers to rank from April 25, 1862. He commanded a brigade with distinction at the Battles of Winchester on May 25 and Cedar Mountain on August 9, 1862. At the Battle of Antietam he succeeded to division command in the 12th Corps until he fell with a severe wound to his right thigh. This wound troubled him for the rest of his life. In May 1863, having sufficiently recovered from his wound to return to field service, he was given command of the Pennsylvania Reserves, which at that time were stationed in the defenses of Washington, D.C. The Reserves were sent to join the Army of the Potomac during the 1863 Confederate invasion of the North, and Crawford commanded the Reserves at Gettysburg, where they fought as a division in the 5th Corps.[3]

43

Crawford served as a division commander with the Army of the Potomac for the rest of the war. He was slightly wounded at Spotsylvania Courthouse on May 8, 1864, and at the Weldon Railroad on August 18, 1864. He was brevetted to major general in the Volunteers on August 1, 1864, and he was brevetted to major general in the Regular Army on March 13, 1865. He was mustered out on June 15, 1866, but he remained in the army, serving as a second lieutenant in the 2nd U.S. Infantry. He was promoted to colonel in February 1869 and he retired in February 1873 because of ongoing problems with his Antietam wound. In Match 1875 he was promoted to brigadier general on the retired list. He lived in Philadelphia and died there.[4]

PHILADELPHIA

LAUREL HILL CEMETERY

GEORGE GORDON MEADE

Born: December 31, 1815
Died: November 6, 1872

General Meade was born in Cadiz, Spain, of American parents. His father was a well-to-do businessman who would later suffer financial troubles. The Meade family moved to Philadelphia in June 1816, although George's father was left behind in a Spanish prison.[1]

Meade received his early education at a military academy in Germantown, Pennsylvania, at the Mount Hope Institution in Baltimore, and at a school in Washington, D.C. run by future Supreme Court Chief Justice Salmon P. Chase. In 1831 Meade was appointed to West Point, graduating in 1835, ranked 19th out of 56. Initially sent to Florida in late 1835, Meade became ill with a fever and was reassigned to the Watertown Arsenal in Massachusetts. In October 1836 he resigned from the army and began a career in engineering.[2]

In May 1842 Meade rejoined the army and for the next four years he served in the Corps of Topographical Engineers. During the Mexican War he served as a topographical engineer at the Battles of Palo Alto, Resaca de la Palma, and Monterey. He received a brevet to first lieutenant for his actions at Monterey. From the end of the war until 1861 he continued to serve as an engineer in the army, rising to the grade of captain.[3]

On August 31, 1861, Meade was commissioned brigadier general of volunteers and he was placed in command of one of the three brigades of Pennsylvania Reserves. The Reserves spent the winter of 1861-1862 in the defenses around Washington, D.C. In June 1862 his brigade was sent to the Peninsula to join the Army of the Potomac. Meade saw action at Mechanicsville and Gaines Mill, but he was severely wounded both in the arm and the side of the back during the fighting at Glendale on June 30, 1862.[4]

Meade quickly returned to field service and he led a brigade at Second Manassas in August. At South Mountain and Antietam he commanded a division in the 1st Corps. He temporarily commanded that corps at Antietam after the wounding of its commander, General Joseph Hooker, despite the fact that Meade was slightly wounded in the thigh. On November 29, 1862, Meade was commissioned major general of volunteers. He led a division at Fredericksburg, where his assault against the Confederate right temporarily pierced the Rebel line; only a lack of support forced Meade's troops to pull back. Meade's attack was the only Union success in an otherwise disastrous battle.[5]

On December 25, 1862, Meade was given command of the 5th Corps. His troops saw limited action at Chancellorsville in May 1863. On June 28, 1863, during the Confederate invasion of the North, Meade was unexpectedly given command of the Army of the Potomac. He performed quite well at the Battle of Gettysburg, where he was willing to fight a defensive battle while his opponent battered the Rebel army against Meade's defensive line. Although he was criticized for not aggressively pursuing the retreating Confederates after the battle, he had finally achieved something no other commander of the Army of the Potomac had before him – a victory over Robert E. Lee.[6]

On July 7, 1863, Meade was rewarded for his victory with a promotion to brigadier general in the Regular Army, to rank from July 3, 1863. The remainder of 1863 was spent in several campaigns in Virginia that involved much maneuvering but little fighting. The next spring Ulysses S. Grant was named lieutenant general in command of all Union forces, and Grant decided to accompany the Army of the Potomac during its 1864-1865 campaign against Lee's Army of Northern Virginia. Although Meade actually remained in command of the Army of the Potomac for the rest of the war, to the general public it was now Grant's army. Also, Grant's decision to accompany the Army of the Potomac created an awkward and cumbersome situation for Meade and Grant regarding the issuance of orders and the planning of strategy and tactics for that army. Through it all Meade performed well and he did his best to cooperate with Grant to make the best of an awkward situation. It is to his credit that Meade did not permit pride or jealousy to interfere with the performance of his duties in 1864-1865.[7]

Meade was promoted to major general in the Regular Army to rank from August 18, 1864. After the war he served as commander of several departments and military divisions in the East. When Grant became President in March 1869, William T. Sherman was named general-in-chief and Phil Sheridan received a promotion to lieutenant general. Meade was greatly disappointed to learn that he had not received the promotion to lieutenant general; Meade felt that he deserved the promotion more than Sheridan, whom he despised. The Glendale wound in the side of his back continued to trouble him and he frequently suffered from bouts of pneumonia and jaundice. He spent his last years in Philadelphia, where he died from pneumonia.[8]

PHILADELPHIA

LAUREL HILL CEMETERY

JAMES ST. CLAIR MORTON

Born: September 24, 1829
Died: June 17, 1864

General Morton was born in Philadelphia. He entered the University of Pennsylvania at the age of 14 and at 18 he entered West Point. He graduated from West Point in 1851, ranked 2nd out of 42. He was assigned to the elite Corps of Engineers, where he worked on a variety of assignments, such as the construction of forts and aqueducts. He taught engineering at West Point from 1855-1857, and in 1860 he was sent to Central America to examine a possible railroad route through the isthmus there. He also wrote several treatises on engineering and fortifications.[1]

From June until October of 1862 Morton was the chief engineer of the Army of the Ohio, and then in October he became the chief engineer of the Army of the Cumberland. At times Morton also served as commander of that army's Pioneer Brigade. On April 4, 1863, he was commissioned brigadier general of volunteers to rank from November 29, 1862. He saw action at Stones River and Chickamauga, and he was slightly wounded at the latter battle. At his request he was mustered out of the volunteer service on November 7, 1863, and so he reverted to his Regular Army grade of major in the Corps of Engineers. He then resumed engineering work in and around Chattanooga and Nashville, and in January 1864 he became an assistant to the chief engineer in Washington.[2]

On May 18, 1864, Morton was named chief engineer for the 9th Corps, and in that capacity he served during the next month with the Army of the Potomac. On June 17, 1864, he was mortally wounded in the chest while performing reconnaissance work at Petersburg preparatory to a Union assault that day. He was posthumously brevetted brigadier general in the Regular Army to date from June 17, 1864.[3]

PHILADELPHIA

LAUREL HILL CEMETERY

HENRY MORRIS NAGLEE

Born: January 15, 1815
Died: March 5, 1886

General Naglee was born in Philadelphia.[1] In 1835 he graduated from West Point, ranked 23rd out of 56. Six months after graduation he resigned from the army and began a career in New York state as a civil engineer. During the Mexican War he was a captain in the 1st New York Volunteers, in command of a company. After mustering out in October 1848, Naglee lived in San Francisco, where he was engaged in banking and he was a member of the California militia.[2]

On May 14, 1861, Naglee was named lieutenant colonel of the 16th U.S. Infantry. He resigned his commission in the Regular Army on January 10, 1862, and he was commissioned brigadier general of volunteers on February 4, 1862. During the winter of 1861-1862, he commanded several brigades stationed in the Washington, D.C. defenses. He saw action during the Peninsula Campaign in the spring of 1862 while commanding several brigades in the 4th Corps in the Army of the Potomac. On May 31, 1862, at Fair Oaks he was wounded four times, once each in the right breast and right shoulder, and twice in the right leg, but these wounds did not necessitate his leaving the field. In December 1862 Naglee was sent to the Department of North Carolina, where at first he commanded a brigade and then a division, and later several districts.[3]

In August 1863 Naglee was given command of the District of Virginia, with his headquarters in Norfolk. Unfortunately he ran into disfavor with the governor of the "Restored Government of Virginia" when he refused to enforce a directive that anyone who was unwilling to take an oath of allegiance to the United States and the restored government should suffer the forfeiture of property. On September 23, 1863, Naglee was relieved of command and sent to Cincinnati to await orders. No further orders came and so on April 4, 1864, he was mustered out.[4]

Naglee spent his last years in California, where he again engaged in banking. Later he owned and operated a vineyard in San Jose. He grew Riesling and Charbonneau grapes to produce a Naglee brandy. He died in San Francisco while visiting his doctor.[5]

PHILADELPHIA

LAUREL HILL CEMETERY

JOSHUA THOMAS OWEN

Born: March 29, 1821
Died: November 7, 1887

General Owen was born in Caermarthen, Wales, but he moved with his family to Baltimore, Maryland, in 1830. He graduated from Jefferson College in 1845. He and his brother founded the Chestnut Hill Academy for Boys in Philadelphia, and he taught at the academy. Owen also practiced law in Philadelphia. From 1857 to 1859 he served in the Pennsylvania Legislature. He was a private in the First City Troop, a local militia unit.[1]

On May 8, 1861, Owen was named colonel of the 24th Pennsylvania, a ninety-day regiment that remained along the Potomac River during the First Manassas Campaign. Soon after the muster out of that regiment, Owen became colonel of the 69th Pennsylvania on August 18, 1861. He saw service in the Army of the Potomac in virtually every battle from Fair Oaks on the Peninsula in May 1862 to Cold Harbor in June 1864. He was appointed brigadier general of volunteers on November 29, 1862, for gallant and meritorious conduct at Glendale. The appointment expired on March 4, 1863, but it was renewed on March 30, 1863. He commanded various brigades and divisions in the 2nd Corps from July 1862 until June 1864.[2]

Owen's record was not spotless, however. He was placed under arrest in late June 1863 while commanding the Philadelphia Brigade on the march to Gettysburg (and thereby did not see any action in that battle), although nothing came of the arrest and Owen returned to command another brigade in August 1863. But after the battle of Cold Harbor in June 1864 he was accused of disobedience of orders in the face of the enemy at both Spotsylvania Courthouse and Cold Harbor, and these charges led to his dismissal from the army on July 18,1864.[3]

Owen returned to Philadelphia and resumed his career as a lawyer. He served as the Recorder of Deeds in Philadelphia from 1866 until 1871. In 1871 he founded the New York Daily Register, which became the official publication of the New York Courts. He worked as a member of the editorial staff of that publication until his death in Philadelphia in 1887.[4]

PHILADELPHIA

LAUREL HILL CEMETERY

FRANCIS ENGLE PATTERSON

Born: May 7, 1821
Died: November 22, 1862

General Patterson was born in Philadelphia.[1] His father was General Robert Patterson, a veteran of the Mexican War who in July 1861 failed in his mission to keep Joseph Johnston's Confederate forces in the Shenandoah Valley from reinforcing the Confederate forces at Manassas during the First Manassas Campaign. Francis attended the University of Pennsylvania. He served in the Mexican War from 1846 to 1847 in McCulloch's Texas Rangers. On June 24, 1847, he became a second lieutenant in the 1st (U.S.) Artillery, and he was promoted to first lieutenant in October 1848. He remained in the army until May 1, 1857, having reached the grade of captain of the 9th Infantry in March 1855. He returned to private life and worked as a merchant.[2]

On April 25, 1861, Patterson was named colonel of the 17th Pennsylvania, a ninety-day regiment. The regiment saw no combat and it was mustered out on August 2, 1861. Patterson was commissioned brigadier general of volunteers on April 11, 1862. He commanded a brigade in the 3rd Corps at Williamsburg and Fair Oaks during the Peninsula Campaign, but he had to temporarily relinquish command during the fighting on June 1, 1862, because of illness. He returned to command of his brigade on June 6, 1862, and continued in command of his brigade throughout the summer and autumn of 1862.[3]

On November 9, 1862, Patterson's division commander, General Daniel E. Sickles, issued a report in which he accused Patterson of ordering a retreat from Catlett's

Station to Bristoe, "without orders, inconsistent with his instructions, and...without sufficient reason." Patterson stated that he retreated because he thought his command was in an untenable position without support and the sound of train whistles led him to believe that enemy troops were approaching his position. Sickles placed Patterson under arrest. The 3rd Corps commander endorsed Sickles' report on November 11 with a recommendation that the matter be investigated, and the army commander concurred with this recommendation on November 24. The investigation never took place, because on November 22, 1862, Patterson was found dead in his tent, killed by the discharge of his pistol. His death was officially recorded as an accident, although suicide has always been suspected because of these circumstances.[4]

PHILADELPHIA

LAUREL HILL CEMETERY

JOHN CLIFFORD PEMBERTON

Born: August 10, 1814
Died: July 13, 1881

General Pemberton was born in Philadelphia and he graduated from West Point in 1837, ranked 27th out of 50. From 1837 to 1839 he served in Florida during the Second Seminole War, and then he spent the next seven years at various posts in Michigan, New York, Virginia, Pennsylvania, and Texas. During the Mexican War he participated in the fighting at Palo Alto and Resaca de la Palma in May 1846. Then in August Pemberton became an aide-de-camp to General William Worth and he served in that capacity for the remainder of the war. He won two brevets (to captain and major) for his conduct at Monterey and Molino del Rey. Between 1848 and 1861 he served at a variety of posts, from Texas to Florida, and he participated in the 1858 Utah expedition.[1]

In 1848 Pemberton married a Virginian and he had become quite partial to Virginia after spending some time stationed at Norfolk. Thus, when Virginia declared itself seceded on April 17, 1861, Pemberton had to resolve his conflicting loyalties between his country, and his wife and adopted state. After some intense soul searching, he resigned from the army on April 24, 1861.[2]

On May 8, 1861, Pemberton was named lieutenant colonel of artillery in the Provisional Army of Virginia. He was commissioned major of artillery in the Confederate Army on June 15, 1861, but he was quickly promoted, being named brigadier general two days later, and major general in January 1862. He commanded the Department of South Carolina, Georgia, and Florida, where his abruptness irritated some local politicians. He was promoted once more to lieutenant general on October 10, 1862, despite his lack of any real combat experience, and he was given command of the Department of Mississippi and East Louisiana. At the time this seemed to be a quiet command, but the important citadel of Vicksburg was in that Department and the Union forces in that area were preparing a campaign to seize Vicksburg. His ultimate defeat in the Vicksburg Campaign the next spring and summer was caused by a combination of his inexperience and ineptitude, General Ulysses S. Grant's brilliance, and the failure of Pemberton's superiors to formulate and carry out a coherent plan.[3]

Pemberton's surrender of Vicksburg on July 4, 1863, led some Southerners to accuse him of treason to the South, based in part on the fact that Pemberton was born in Pennsylvania. There is no evidence at all to support such accusations. Pemberton's military experience was almost exclusively with staff, and not combat, positions, and he was simply in over his head in this campaign. After his exchange, Pemberton proved to be an embarrassment for the Confederate government, for they could not or would not find him a command appropriate for a lieutenant general.[4]

Finally in May 1864 Pemberton resigned his lieutenant general commission, and he served the Confederacy for the rest of the war as a lieutenant colonel of artillery and an inspector of artillery and ordinance. After the war he farmed near Warrenton, Virginia, and then he moved back to Philadelphia, where he died.[5]

PHILADELPHIA

LAUREL HILL CEMETERY

CHARLES FERGUSON SMITH

Born: April 24, 1807
Died: April 25, 1862

General Smith was born in Philadelphia, the son of an army surgeon. In 1825 he graduated from West Point at the age of 18, ranked 19th out of 37. After spending several years in typical garrison duty, he returned to West Point to be an instructor and adjutant, and from 1838 until 1843 he served as the Commandant of Cadets. During the Mexican War he saw extensive service and he distinguished himself on many battlefields, earning three brevets (major, lieutenant colonel, and colonel). After the war he served on the frontier and he participated in the Utah Expedition involving the Mormons. He commanded the Department of Utah from February 1860 until February 1861.[1]

In April 1861 Smith, a lieutenant colonel in the Regular Army, served briefly as commander of the Department of Washington, but he was soon sent to New York for recruiting duties. On August 31, 1861, he was commissioned brigadier general of volunteers, and on September 9, 1861, he was named colonel in the Regular Army.[2]

Smith commanded the District of Western Kentucky from September 1861 through January 1862. He then commanded the 2nd Division of General Ulysses S. Grant's army in the operations against Forts Henry and Donelson in February 1862. He personally led the charge of his division on February 15 that halted the Confederate escape from Fort Donelson and led to the surrender of the fort to Grant the next day.[3]

Smith was promoted to major general of volunteers on March 21, 1862. Earlier that month Grant was removed from command of the Army of the Tennessee, because of a dispute between Grant and his superior officer, General Henry Halleck, and Smith was given command of the army. The army was moved south to camps at Pittsburg Landing, on the banks of the Tennessee River, in preparation for an advance into Mississippi. On March 12 Smith badly scraped his shin when he jumped into a ship. His shin was cut nearly to the bone, from the ankle to the knee. The wound became infected and Smith had to relinquish command of the army to Grant. Smith's condition worsened and he died on April 25 at Savannah, Tennessee, in his sickbed.[4]

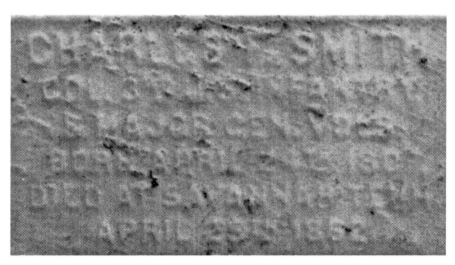

PHILADELPHIA

LAUREL HILL CEMETERY

ALFRED SULLY

Born: May 22, 1820
Died: April 27, 1879

General Sully was born in Philadelphia.[1] His father was the famous painter Thomas Sully. In his youth Alfred showed an interest in mechanics and engineering, and so he was enrolled at West Point. He graduated in 1841, ranked 34th out of 52. Because of his low rank, he was assigned to the infantry rather than the topographical engineers. Sully was sent to Florida, where he saw action involving the Seminoles. Then he was assigned to garrison duty on the Great Lakes. In 1847 he participated in the siege of Vera Cruz during the Mexican War. Next he was sent to California for more garrison duty, where he was the regimental quartermaster for several years. In 1852 he was promoted to captain and he was sent to the mid-west for more garrison duty, mainly in Minnesota and Nebraska Territories. During these years in the mid-west Sully was involved in fighting against various Indian tribes, most notably the Cheyennes.[2]

In the early months of the Civil War Sully served in northern Missouri. In November 1861 he was sent to Washington, D.C., where he served as provost marshal of Georgetown. On March 4, 1862, Sully was named colonel of the 1st Minnesota and the regiment was assigned to the Army of the Potomac. Sully was slightly wounded on his ear at Fair Oaks on June 1, 1862, and he commanded a 2nd Corps brigade throughout the Peninsula Campaign. At Antietam Sully was again in command of the 1st Minnesota. His performance in these campaigns earned him a commission as brigadier general of volunteers on September 26, 1862. He led a brigade in the 2nd Corps at Fredericksburg and Chancellorsville, but that would be his last combat against the Confederates. Shortly after the latter battle he was given command of the District of Dakota. The Sioux Indians in Minnesota had staged an uprising in 1862, and an experienced Indian fighter such as Sully was needed to help bring the situation under control. For the next several years Sully was engaged in fighting local Indians in Minnesota and the Dakotas, and he enhanced his reputation as an effective Indian fighter. At the end of the war he received brevets to major general of volunteers and brigadier general in the Regular Army.[3]

Sully mustered out in April 1866, but he decided to remain in the army and in July 1866 he was promoted to lieutenant colonel of the 3rd U.S. Infantry. He served at various frontier posts, rising to colonel of the 21st U.S. Infantry in 1873. Unfortunately his service on the frontier after the Civil War was frequently interrupted by various health problems, such as fever and rheumatism. He was in command of Fort Vancouver, Washington, when he died.[4]

PHILADELPHIA

LAUREL HILL CEMETERY

HECTOR TYNDALE

Born: March 24, 1821
Died: March 19, 1880

General Tyndale was born in Philadelphia.[1] His father was an Irish immigrant who became a very successful importer of glass and china. He was offered an appointment to West Point, but it was declined at his Quaker mother's request, and so he joined his father's business. With the death of his father in 1845, Tyndale and his brother-in-law created their own glass and china import business. Tyndale acquired a reputation as an expert regarding ceramics and porcelain. In 1859 he accompanied John Brown's wife when she came to Charlestown, (West) Virginia for a final visit before John Brown's execution. Tyndale helped escort the abolitionist's body back to Lake Placid, New York, for burial. His motivation was concern for Mrs. Brown's safety and not support for John Brown's cause.[2]

At the start of the Civil War Tyndale was in Paris on business. Soon after his return to America, he was named major of the 28th Pennsylvania on June 28, 1861. The regiment was assigned to the Harpers Ferry area. He was promoted to lieutenant colonel on April 25, 1862. The regiment saw action in May 1862 during the Shenandoah Valley Campaign, and at Cedar Mountain and Second Manassas later that year. Tyndale commanded a brigade in the 12th Corps at Antietam, despite the fact that he was only a lieutenant colonel.   He displayed great bravery in this battle, having three horses shot from under him. He was also wounded in both the head and the hip. The head wound fractured his skull, and at first it was believed to be a fatal wound, but he recovered.[3]

Tyndale was commissioned brigadier general of volunteers on April 9, 1863, effective November 29, 1862. Although he technically returned to duty in May 1863, he was unable to immediately return to field command due to complications from his head wound. Between July 13 and September 19 he commanded a brigade in the 11th Corps, but he was too weak to continue in command and so he was sent home to recuperate. On October 19 he resumed command of his brigade and he led it during the Chattanooga Campaign that autumn. Between February and April 1864 he commanded an 11th Corps division. On April 16 Tyndale was given command of a brigade in the 20th Corps, but illness forced him to apply for a leave of absence on May 2, 1864, just before the Atlanta Campaign began. He returned to Philadelphia, but health woes forced him to resign on August 26, 1864. In March 1865 he was brevetted major general of volunteers.[4]

Tyndale resumed his work in the import business in Philadelphia. He was active in local politics, although in 1868 he lost the race for mayor of Philadelphia. He was also a supporter of various local educational institutions, including the University of Pennsylvania. He died in Philadelphia.[5]

Laurel Hill Cemetery is located at 3822 Ridge Avenue, near Fairmount Park on the east side of the Schuylkill River. As marked on the map, Bohlen's grave is in Section Y, Crawford's and Meade's graves are in Section L, Morton's grave is in Section G, Naglee's grave is in Section 1, Owen's grave is in Section 5, Patterson's grave is in Section K, Pemberton's grave is in Section 9, Smith's grave is in Section X, Sully's grave is in Section A, and Tyndale's grave is in Section H.

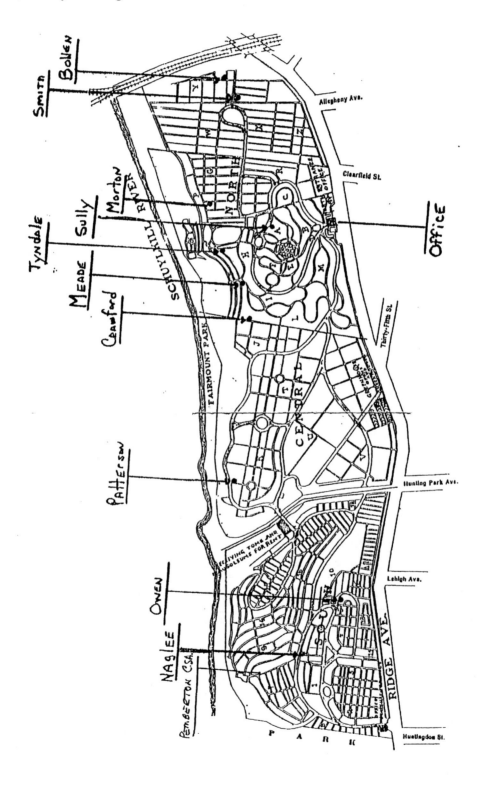

64

PHILADELPHIA

PHILADELPHIA NATIONAL CEMETERY

GALUSHA PENNYPACKER

Born: June 1, 1844
Died: October 1, 1916

General Pennypacker was born in Chester County, Pennsylvania near the Valley Forge encampment site. His mother died when he was four years old and his father moved to California, and so young Pennypacker was raised by his grandmother in the house George Washington had used as his headquarters during the Valley Forge encampment.[1]

Pennypacker was not quite 17 when the Civil War began, but he quickly enlisted in a ninety-day regiment and became its quartermaster sergeant on April 22, 1861. After that regiment's muster out on July 29, he recruited a company of the 97th Pennsylvania and was named its captain on August 22, 1861. In October 1861 he was promoted to major, at the age of 17. He spent the next two years in the Department of the South, seeing action in Florida and at Fort Wagner in the Charleston area.[2]

In the spring of 1864 the 97th Pennsylvania was transferred to General Benjamin Butler's Army of the James, and on April 3, 1864, Pennypacker was promoted to lieutenant colonel. On May 20, 1864, he gallantly led the charge of his regiment at Green Plains, Virginia. He received two minor wounds in the knee and chest, but a third, more serious wound to his right elbow forced him to leave the field. After convalescing in a hospital and at home, Pennypacker returned to his regiment in August. He was commissioned colonel on August 15, 1864, at the age of 20. He served with distinction in the various battles near Petersburg, receiving a wound in his right ankle at Fort Gilmer in September. At times he commanded brigades in the 10th and 24th Corps.[3]

Pennypacker participated in Butler's failed assault against Fort Fisher near Wilmington, North Carolina in December 1864, and on January 15, 1865, he led his brigade in the successful assault against that bastion. His bravery nearly cost him his life, for he suffered a severe wound in his right side and hip during the assault that required ten months hospitalization at Fort Monroe and further convalescence at home. In 1891 he was awarded the Medal of Honor for his gallantry at Fort Fisher.[4]

On April 28, 1865, Pennypacker was commissioned brigadier general of volunteers to rank from February 18, 1865. Thus he became the youngest commissioned full rank Union general in the war at the age of 20. He was later brevetted major general of volunteers on March 13, 1865, and in 1867 he was brevetted major general in the Regular Army. He continued to serve in the army, mainly on the frontier, and on July 28, 1866, he was promoted to colonel. On July 3, 1883, he retired from the army. He died in Philadelphia.[5]

The Philadelphia National Cemetery is located at the intersection of Haines Street and Limekiln Pike, in the northern part of the city. Upon entering the cemetery, park near the flagpole. Pennypacker's distinctive private grave marker is in the Officers Section, which is in the middle of the cemetery.

PHILADELPHIA

ST. DOMINIC'S CHURCHYARD

THOMAS KILBY SMITH

Born: September 23, 1820
Died: December 14, 1887

General Smith was born in Dorchester, Massachusetts, but he grew up on a farm in Ohio. He graduated from Cincinnati College in 1837 and he studied law under Salmon P. Chase, the future Supreme Court Chief Justice. Smith held several federal positions prior to the war, such as a clerkship in the Post Office Department in Washington, D.C. and U.S. Marshal for the southern district in Ohio.[1]

On September 9, 1861, Smith became lieutenant colonel of the 54th Ohio and on October 31 he became colonel of the regiment. His regiment was actively engaged in the Shiloh, Corinth, and Vicksburg Campaigns. At various times between April 1862 and May 1863 Smith temporarily commanded several different brigades. Then during the summer of 1863 he served on General Ulysses S. Grant's staff. On August 11, 1863, he was commissioned brigadier general of volunteers and in September 1863 he resumed command of a brigade. He performed well in command of the provisional division during the Red River Campaign in the spring of 1864 despite the fact that the campaign itself was an utter failure. At the end of that campaign he was forced to take a leave of absence, being afflicted with malarial fever, and he spent the remainder of 1864 convalescing at home in Ohio.[2]

In March 1865 Smith was named commander of the District of Florida and Southern Alabama, but continuing health problems forced him to take another leave of absence in August 1865. He was brevetted major general of volunteers on March 13,

1865. Smith left the army in January 1866 and in 1867 he accepted the post of U.S. Consul to Panama, partially in hopes of regaining his health.   He returned to the U.S. in 1869 because of his ongoing health problems. He took up residence in Torresdale, which was then a suburb of Philadelphia, but he was a virtual invalid because of his poor health. In 1887 he moved to New York City and two years later he died there in a hospital.[3]

St. Dominic's Churchyard is located at 8504 Frankford Avenue (U.S. Route 13) in the former suburb of Torresdale, which is now a part of northeast Philadelphia.   Smith's distinctive grave marker can be easily found a short distance behind the church.

SACRED TO THE MEMORY
of
THOMAS KILBY SMITH
BREVET MAJOR GENERAL
of
UNITED STATES VOLUNTEERS
1861—1866
BORN IN BOSTON MASS
23 SEPTEMBER 1820
DIED IN NEW YORK CITY
14 DECEMBER 1887

REQUIESCAT IN PACE

PHILADELPHIA

ST. JAMES THE LESS CHURCHYARD

JAMES BARNET FRY

Born: February 22, 1827
Died: July 11, 1894

General Fry was born in Carrollton, Illinois.[1] He graduated from West Point in 1847, ranked 14th out of 38. He then taught artillery at the Academy, served in the Mexican War, and performed garrison duty in Mexico City after the war. After several years of serving on the frontier, he was adjutant at West Point between 1854 and 1859. He was a member of the force sent to Harpers Ferry to suppress John Brown's raid in October 1859.[2]

In early 1861 Fry was in command of a battery of light artillery in the defenses of Washington, D.C., but beginning in March 1861 and continuing throughout the entire four years of the Civil War he served as a staff officer. On May 31, 1861, he was named chief of staff and assistant adjutant general for the Union army being amassed at Washington, D.C., which would eventually become the Army of the Potomac. He served in that capacity for General Irvin McDowell's army during the First Manassas Campaign, and he continued in that capacity until November 12, 1861. Three days later he was named chief of staff and assistant adjutant general for General Don Carlos Buell's Department of the Ohio and he served there until October 30, 1862. Next he served for several months as Assistant Adjutant General in Washington. Then on March 17, 1863, he was named colonel in the Regular Army and Provost Marshal General, a post he held for the remainder of the war. In the latter position he oversaw efforts to suppress desertions, reorganize recruiting, and enforce conscription. He performed these duties admirably and on April 21, 1864, he was made a brigadier general in the Regular Army. He was brevetted major general in the Regular Army on March 13, 1865.[3]

Fry remained the Provost Marshal General until the bureau was dissolved in 1866. He remained in the army and in March 1875 he was promoted to colonel in the adjutant general's department. Poor health forced him to retire from the army on July 1, 1881. Between 1875 and 1893 he published many writings on various military subjects. He died in Newport, Rhode Island.[4]

St. James The Less Churchyard is located at 3227 West Clearfield Street, just off of Hunting Park Avenue (U.S. Route 13), near Laurel Hill Cemetery. Parke's grave is near the back of the church. When you are facing Parke's grave, Fry's grave is behind you and to your right, next to the path in the churchyard. A cenotaph for CSA Brig. Gen. Alexander W. Reynolds is next to the church, a short distance from Parke's grave.

PHILADELPHIA

ST. JAMES THE LESS CHURCHYARD

JOHN GRUBB PARKE

Born: September 22, 1827
Died: December 16, 1900

General Parke was born near Coatesville, Pennsylvania, but he grew up in Philadelphia. After attending both a private academy and the University of Pennsylvania, Parke enrolled at West Point in 1845. He graduated in 1849, ranked 2nd out of 43, and based on his high graduation rank he received an assignment with the topographical engineers. He spent the pre-Civil War years on various engineering projects for the army, such as railroad surveying and construction projects at rivers and harbors, in such diverse places as California, Minnesota, and New Mexico and Washington Territories. He was promoted to first lieutenant in 1856.[1]

On September 9, 1861, Parke became a captain of engineers. He returned to the East from Washington Territory in October 1861 and he was commissioned brigadier general of volunteers on November 23, 1861. Parke commanded a brigade in General Ambrose Burnside's North Carolina Expedition, seeing action at Roanoke Island and New Bern. On July 18, 1862, he was commissioned major general of volunteers. During the Antietam Campaign Parke served as Burnside's chief of staff. Parke remained Burnside's chief of staff during the latter's short and unsuccessful tenure as commander of the Army of the Potomac, from November 7, 1862, until January 25, 1863.[2]

When Burnside was placed in charge of the Department of the Ohio in March 1863, Parke took command of the 9th Corps. He ably led the corps in the Vicksburg Campaign. In the spring of 1864 Parke resumed his service as chief of staff for Burnside when the 9th Corps was again, under Burnside's command, serving with the Army of the Potomac. On August 14, 1864, Parke was again given command of the 9th Corps upon the dismissal of Burnside during the Petersburg siege. He won distinction with his repulse of the Confederate attack at Fort Stedman on March 25, 1865. He was brevetted brigadier and major general in the Regular Army on March 13, 1865.[3]

After Parke mustered out in January 1866, he remained in the army. For the next 21 years he served in the engineers and received promotions to lieutenant colonel in 1879 and colonel in 1884. From 1887 to 1889 he served as superintendent at West Point. He retired in 1889 and died in Washington.[4]

(See directions for grave site on page 70.)

PHILADELPHIA

WISTAR INSTITUTE OF ANATOMY

ISAAC JONES WISTAR

Born: November 14, 1827
Died: September 18, 1905

General Wistar was born in Philadelphia and attended Haverford College. In his youth he worked in a dry goods store and as a mule driver on a canal boat. In 1849 he joined a group going to California to find gold. After working in California as a miner, farmer, mountain man, Indian fighter, and trapper, he studied law and in 1854 he opened a law office in San Francisco. At one point, in Panama, he won a fortune but then lost it at gambling. Eventually he ended up in Philadelphia, where he worked as an attorney.[1]

At the start of the Civil War Wistar recruited a company of volunteers which became a part of the 71st Pennsylvania. Wistar was appointed the regiment's lieutenant colonel on June 28, 1861, and he participated in the disastrous Battle of Ball's Bluff, Virginia, on October 21, 1861. In that battle the regiment's colonel, Edwin D. Baker, was killed, and Wistar became the regiment's commander. He was commissioned colonel as of November 11, 1861. At Ball's Bluff he suffered minor wounds to his jaw and thigh, and a severe wound to his right arm that resulted in the arm being permanently locked at the elbow.[2]

Wistar was able to join the Army of the Potomac at the beginning of the Peninsula Campaign, but in April at Yorktown he contracted typhoid fever and he had to be sent home to recover. He was able to return to the field in August. At the Battle of Antietam on September 17, 1862, Wistar suffered a serious wound that disabled his left arm. On

March 16, 1863, he was commissioned brigadier general of volunteers to date from November 29, 1862, and in May 1863 he had sufficiently recovered from his Antietam wound to command a brigade at Suffolk, Virginia. He participated in several small engagements in that area, although he was frequently ill with fever. Finally in May 1864 Wistar's considerable health problems resulted in his replacement by Colonel Griffin Stedman, and on September 15, 1864, Wistar resigned.[3]

After the war Wistar practiced law, became active in the coal business, managed the state canal system for the Pennsylvania Railroad, served as president of the Academy of Natural Sciences and the American Philosophical Society, and led efforts to sponsor and support museums. In the 1890's he founded The Wistar Institute of Anatomy and Biology. Wistar died at his summer home in Claymont, Delaware. His brain and right arm were removed for scientific study and the remainder of his body was cremated. The urn containing the cremains is on display at the Wistar Institute.[4]

The Wistar Institute of Anatomy is located at 36th and Spruce Streets near the University of Pennsylvania in the western part of the city. The urn containing Wistar's cremains is on display in a showcase on the second floor of the Institute. You will have to contact the Institute to make arrangements to view the urn.

PHILADELPHIA

WOODLANDS CEMETERY

JOHN JOSEPH ABERCROMBIE

Born: March 4, 1798
Died: January 3, 1877

General Abercrombie was born in Baltimore.[1] Little is known of his early life, with some sources even stating that he was born in Tennessee.[2] He graduated from West Point in 1822, ranked 37th out of 40. For the next 47 years he served in the U.S. Army, slowly gaining promotions to second lieutenant in 1822, first lieutenant in 1828, captain in 1836, major in 1847, and lieutenant colonel in 1852. He saw action in the Black Hawk War, the Second Seminole War, and the Mexican War, earning brevet promotions for both the Seminole War and the Mexican War. He was wounded at the Battle of Monterey in the Mexican War. On February 25, 1861, just before the start of the Civil War, he was promoted to colonel.[3]

In June 1861 Abercrombie commanded a brigade in the Department of Pennsylvania, and from July 19 until August 17 he commanded a brigade in the Department of the Shenandoah. He was commissioned brigadier general of volunteers on August 31, 1861. From August 1861 until March 1862 he commanded a brigade in General Nathaniel Banks' division in the Shenandoah Valley. Between March and May 1862 he commanded several different brigades in the Army of the Potomac. During the Peninsula Campaign he commanded a 4th Corps brigade and he saw action at Fair Oaks, where he was dazed upon receiving a slight wound in the head, and at Malvern Hill.[4]

Abercrombie commanded a 4th Corps division from July 12 until August 12, 1862, but that would be his last field command in the war. He commanded a division in the defenses of Washington, D.C. from October 1862 until June 1863, and then he served on various military boards and commissions. In May and June of 1864 Abercrombie commanded several different posts and depots in the Fredericksburg, Virginia area. On June 24, 1864, he was mustered out and on March 13, 1865, he was brevetted brigadier general in the Regular Army. He retired on June 12, 1865, although he served on numerous courts-martial until 1869. He then lived in Roslyn, Long Island, New York, where he died. Originally buried in Jersey City, New Jersey, his remains were reburied at the Woodlands Cemetery in Philadelphia in 1887.[5]

PHILADELPHIA

WOODLANDS CEMETERY

DAVID BELL BIRNEY

Born: May 29, 1825
Died: October 18, 1864

General Birney was born in Huntsville, Alabama, a son of the abolitionist leader and twice unsuccessful anti-slavery Liberal Party presidential candidate James G. Birney and a brother of Union full rank General William Birney. His father's strong feelings about slavery caused him to move the family to Cincinnati in 1838. David graduated from Andover Academy. Later the family lived in Michigan, but health problems led David to move to Pennsylvania in 1848. In Pennsylvania he studied law and in 1856 he began a successful career as a lawyer in Philadelphia.[1]

Birney recruited the 23rd Pennsylvania, a three-month regiment known as Birney's Zouaves, and he became its lieutenant colonel on April 21, 1861. When the regiment enlisted for three years he became its colonel on August 31. On February 17, 1862, he was commissioned brigadier general of volunteers, and he commanded a 3rd Corps brigade at Fair Oaks, Virginia, on May 31, 1862. The next day he was relieved of his command by his corps commander, General Samuel Heintzelman, on allegations of disobeying an order, but Birney was acquitted in a subsequent court-martial. Birney was back in command of his brigade during the Seven Days Battles, winning the praises of his division commander, General Phil Kearny. Birney led his brigade at Second Manassas, and upon the death of Kearny on September 1, 1862, at Chantilly, Virginia, Birney became division commander. He led the division until March 1864, while occasionally having temporary command of the 3rd Corps. On May 20, 1863, he was promoted to major general of volunteers. He was a competent division commander, considering his lack of prior military experience.[2]

       With the break up of the 3rd Corps in March 1864, Birney was given command of a 2nd Corps division. He received a slight wound from a shell fragment at Spotsylvania Courthouse on May 12, 1864. On July 23, 1864, Birney was placed in command of the 10th Corps, but shortly thereafter he contracted malaria, or possibly typhoid fever. His condition worsened and on October 9, 1864, he was sent home to recuperate. He died at his home in Philadelphia nine days later.[3]

The Woodlands Cemetery is located at 4000 Woodland Avenue in the southwestern part of the city. As marked on the map, Abercrombie's grave is in Section H, near the road in the cemetery, and Birney's grave is in the Central Circle Section, next to the road.

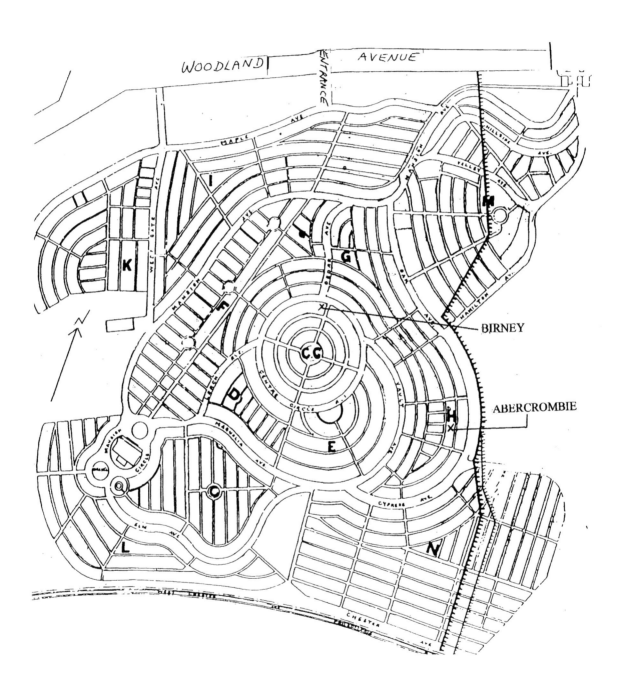

PITTSBURGH

ALLEGHENY CEMETERY

ALEXANDER HAYS

Born: July 8, 1819
Died: May 5, 1864

General Hays was born in Franklin, Pennsylvania. He attended several academies and Allegheny College before entering West Point, where he graduated in 1844, ranked 20th out of 25. After serving on the frontier, Hays saw action during the Mexican War. He was wounded in the leg at Resaca de la Palma and earned a brevet promotion to first lieutenant. On April 12, 1848, he resigned from the army and upon his return to Franklin he engaged in an iron business that soon failed. In 1849 he went to California seeking gold, but he returned to Pennsylvania in 1851. For the next ten years he worked in western Pennsylvania as a construction engineer, building bridges.[1]

In April 1861 Hays was a captain in the Pennsylvania militia and then a major in the 12th Pennsylvania, a three-month regiment recruited in Pittsburgh. On May 14, 1861, Hays was named captain of the 16th U.S. Infantry and on October 9, 1861, he became colonel of the 63rd Pennsylvania. The regiment spent the winter of 1861-1862 in the defenses of Washington, D.C. The next spring he led his regiment during the Peninsula Campaign, and he received two brevet promotions for his gallantry in that campaign. In July 1862 he went on sick leave for blindness in his right eye and partial paralysis in his left arm, but a month later he was back in command of his regiment. In August 1862 Hays was seriously wounded in the leg at Second Manassas and he was commissioned brigadier general of volunteers on September 29, 1862.[2]

After his recovery from his wound, Hays served in the Washington, D.C. defenses during the winter of 1862-1863. Then in late June 1863 he was given command of a 2nd Corps division. He ably led this division at Gettysburg and it was one of the two divisions that successfully bore the brunt of Pickett's Charge and repulsed the Confederate assault. With the merging of the 3rd Corps with the 2nd Corps the next spring, Hays lost command of his division based on seniority. Thus he was in command of a 2nd Corps brigade when the Overland Campaign began in May 1864. Early in the fighting in the Wilderness on May 5 Hays was shot in the head and he died instantly. He was posthumously brevetted major general of volunteers to date from May 5.[3]

PITTSBURGH

ALLEGHENY CEMETERY

CONRAD FEGER JACKSON

Born: September 11, 1813
Died: December 13, 1862

General Jackson was born in Berks County, Pennsylvania. In his youth he was active in the local militia, serving as a lieutenant and adjutant of the Reading Artillerists militia. Jackson saw action as a captain in the Pennsylvania Infantry during the Mexican War. After the war he worked as an agent for the United States Revenue Service. Later he worked as an agent for the Philadelphia & Reading Railroad while living in Pittsburgh. He participated in the local militia in Pittsburgh, rising to captain of the City Guard militia.[1]

The City Guard militia was mustered into the 9th Pennsylvania Reserves on July 27, 1861, and Jackson was named the regiment's colonel. He saw limited action at Dranesville, Virginia on December 20, 1861. The regiment was assigned to the 5th Corps and it was heavily engaged during the Peninsula Campaign. At Glendale on June 30, 1862, Jackson assumed command of his brigade in the absence of its commander, General Truman Seymour, and he continued to command the brigade throughout the remainder of the Peninsula Campaign. Jackson was commissioned brigadier general of volunteers to rank from July 17, 1862. He remained in command of his brigade of Pennsylvania Reserves during the fighting at Second Manassas, until illness forced him to relinquish his command on August 30. This illness prevented Jackson from returning to the field until October 1862, thereby resulting in his missing the Antietam Campaign.[2]

On October 2, 1862, Jackson was given command of a brigade in General George Meade's division of the 1st Corps of the Army of the Potomac. During the battle of Fredericksburg on December 13, 1862, Meade's division launched a furious attack against the Confederate right. During the fighting Jackson's horse was shot from under him, and so he led his brigade forward on foot. Shortly thereafter he was shot in the head above the right eye and died instantly. His body was not recovered until several days later. His original, weathered grave marker was replaced on May 30, 1994, with an exact duplicate.[3]

PITTSBURGH

ALLEGHENY CEMETERY

JAMES SCOTT NEGLEY

Born: December 22, 1826
Died: August 7, 1901

General Negley was born in East Liberty, a hamlet near Pittsburgh, Pennsylvania. He graduated from Western University of Pennsylvania (now Pittsburgh University) in 1846. On December 16, 1846, he enlisted in the 1st Pennsylvania Infantry as a private and he saw action in the Mexican War. He was promoted to sergeant in 1847 and on July 25, 1848, he was mustered out of the army. After the war Negley was active in the local militia in Pittsburgh and he also gained notoriety in the field of gardening.[1]

At the start of the Civil War Negley was a brigadier general in the Pennsylvania militia and he was involved in organizing volunteers in the Pittsburgh area. Between June 10 and July 20, 1861, he commanded a brigade in the Department of Pennsylvania under General Robert Patterson. He was commissioned brigadier general of volunteers to rank from October 1, 1861. From October 5, 1861, until October 10, 1863, he commanded several different brigades and divisions in the Army of the Ohio and the Army of the Cumberland. When the Confederates invaded Kentucky in the fall of 1862, Negley commanded the Union forces left behind to defend Nashville, and so he missed seeing action at the Battle of Perryville on October 8. His performance commanding a division at the Battle of Stone's River earned him a promotion to major general of volunteers as of November 29, 1862.[2]

Negley's rise through the ranks came to an abrupt halt with the Battle of Chickamauga on September 19-20, 1863. He commanded a division that was in the thick of the fighting on both days of the battle. At the end of the battle several fellow officers accused him of cowardice and desertion of his command when he and a part of his division (along with much of the Union army) was routed from the field on the second day of the battle. A Court of Inquiry was convened, at Negley's request, in January and February of 1864. On February 23, 1864, the Court issued a "Finding and Opinion" wherein the Court exonerated him, complimented him on the "zeal" he displayed in discharging his duties in the battle, and strongly criticized one of his accusers. Although he was cleared of all charges, his military career was basically finished. During the remainder of 1864 he served on several boards and commanded a draft rendezvous in the North, but it was obvious he was not going to receive any further field commands. So on January 19, 1865, Negley resigned from the army. For the rest of his life he blamed his fate on the prejudice West Pointers had against civilian officers.[3]

Negley returned to Pittsburgh and he entered politics three years later by winning election to Congress as a Republican in 1868. He was a U.S. Representative from Pennsylvania from March 1869 until March 1875, and from March 1885 until March 1887. When not serving in Congress, Negley was busy working as the president of a railroad in New York. He died in Plainfield, New Jersey.[4]

PITTSBURGH

ALLEGHENY CEMETERY

THOMAS ALGEO ROWLEY

Born: October 5, 1808
Died: May 14, 1892

General Rowley was born in Pittsburgh.[1] Prior to the Mexican War he worked as a cabinetmaker and he was elected justice of the peace. He served during the Mexican War as a captain in the Jackson Blues, a company of Pennsylvania volunteers. After he was mustered out on July 18, 1848, he returned to Pittsburgh and became very active in local politics. He worked as a contractor for the city and from 1857-1860 he served as clerk of courts for Allegheny County.[2]

Rowley became colonel of the 13th Pennsylvania Infantry, a three-month regiment, on April 25, 1861. The regiment saw no combat, being deployed on garrison duty near the Potomac River. The regiment re-enlisted as the 102nd Pennsylvania, and on August 6, 1861, Rowley was named colonel of the regiment. Assigned to the 4th Corps, the regiment saw considerable action during the Peninsula Campaign of 1862. On May 31, 1862, at Seven Pines, Rowley received a wound to the back of his head that fractured the left side of his skull and severely stunned him. The wound was treated at a field hospital and he continued to lead his regiment throughout the remainder of the campaign. His brigade commander commended Rowley for refusing to quit his regiment despite his severe wound. After Second Manassas the regiment covered the retreat of the Union army at Chantilly and it was in reserve at Antietam. The regiment was then reassigned to the 6th Corps. Rowley was commissioned brigadier general of volunteers as of November 29, 1862.[3]

In November 1862 Rowley was given command of a brigade in the 6th Corps and he led the brigade at the Battle of Fredericksburg. Then in March 1863 Rowley was given command of a new brigade of Pennsylvania infantry, which was assigned to the 1st Corps. Rowley commanded the brigade at Chancellorsville, but his green troops saw no action in that battle. On July 1, 1863, Rowley temporarily commanded a 1st Corps division during the first day's fighting at Gettysburg and on July 3 he was slightly wounded by several spent shell fragments. Almost immediately after the battle accusations were voiced, alleging that Rowley had been intoxicated on the battlefield on July 1. In September 1863 he was on sick leave with a fever, and on October 14, 1863, he was assigned to Portland, Maine, to command a depot for drafted men. [4]

From April 23-29, 1864, a court-martial was convened concerning Rowley's conduct at Gettysburg. He was convicted of drunkenness and improper conduct at Gettysburg; however, Secretary of War Edwin M. Stanton restored Rowley to duty, citing conflicts in the testimony. Rowley reported for duty to the Army of the Potomac in June 1864, but General Ulysses S. Grant quickly issued an order, directing Rowley to proceed to Washington, D.C. for further orders. Grant's order stated that there was a feeling in the Army of the Potomac of distrust of Rowley's fitness to command troops in the field. Rowley was sent to Pittsburgh to command the District of the Monongahela. He resigned from the army on December 29, 1864.[5]

Rowley lived in Pittsburgh the rest of his life, where he practiced law, worked as a contractor, and served as a U.S. marshal. The Seven Pines wound troubled him for the remainder of his life; by the 1870s he was partially blind in his left eye and he experienced tremendous pain in the left side of his head. He died in Pittsburgh.[6]

PITTSBURGH

ALLEGHENY CEMETERY

DAVID HENRY WILLIAMS

Born: March 19, 1819
Died: June 1, 1891

General Williams was born and raised on a farm in Otsego County, New York. After studying civil engineering in his local schools, he moved to Detroit in 1837 to work as a railroad surveyor. He was engaged in this work in Michigan for the next ten years. It is reported that he served in the Mexican War, although not as an officer, but details are lacking as to the unit he served in or the time frame of his service in the war.[1] After the war he moved to Pittsburgh, where he continued to work as a civil engineer and railroad surveyor. Williams was also active in the local militia in Pittsburgh.[2]

On July 23, 1861, Williams was named colonel of the 82nd Pennsylvania. All of the companies in this regiment were from Philadelphia, except Williams' company from Pittsburgh. The regiment was assigned to the 4th Corps and it saw considerable action during the Peninsula Campaign of 1862, particularly at Seven Pines and Malvern Hill. After seeing minimal combat at the Battle of Antietam on September 17, 1862, the regiment was reassigned to the 6th Corps. The regiment was lightly engaged at Fredericksburg on December 13, 1862.[3]

On November 29, 1862, Williams was appointed brigadier general of volunteers, but the commission expired on March 4, 1863, based on the Senate failing to act upon his nomination. Shortly afterwards he resigned from the army and returned to Pittsburgh, where he resumed his work as a civil engineer. He also taught engineering in Pittsburgh. Unfortunately, health problems soon ended his careers in civil engineering and teaching.

Williams was soon an invalid, but he found work as a writer for magazines and newspapers. He died in Allegheny, which is now a part of Pittsburgh. At his grave site there is no individual marker for him, only the large family marker inscribed with the word "Williams." [4]

Allegheny Cemetery is located at 4734 Butler Street, in the northern part of Pittsburgh. As marked on the map, Hays' grave is in Section 8 (next to the road), Jackson's grave is in Section 31 (next to the road), Negley's grave is in Section 19 (next to the road), Rowley's grave is in Section 7 (not visible from the road), and Williams' grave is in Section 16 (near the road).

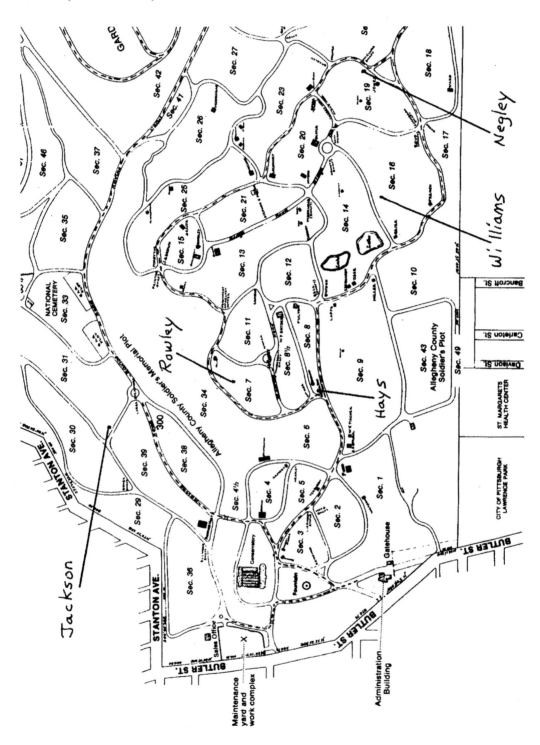

90

POTTSVILLE

PRESBYTERIAN CEMETERY

JAMES NAGLE

Born: April 5, 1822
Died: August 22, 1866

General Nagle was born in Reading, Pennsylvania and his family moved to Pottsville when he was thirteen. He worked as a painter and paperhanger, which had been his father's trade. In 1842 he organized the Washington Artillery militia unit, which later served as a part of the 1st Pennsylvania during the Mexican War. Nagle saw action in the war as a captain in the 1st Pennsylvania from December 15, 1846, until he was mustered out of the army on July 27, 1848.[1]

On April 22, 1861, Nagle became colonel of the 6th Pennsylvania, a three-month regiment. Although the regiment was not mustered into the Federal service, it did serve in General Robert Patterson's force in the Shenandoah Valley. After the regiment was mustered out on July 26, 1861, Nagle recruited and organized the 48th Pennsylvania and became the regiment's colonel on October 1, 1861. Nagle commanded a brigade in North Carolina between April and July 1862. He then led a 9th Corps brigade in the Second Manassas Campaign and he was appointed brigadier general of volunteers on September 10, 1862. He continued to lead his brigade at South Mountain and Antietam in September 1862. At the latter battle his brigade successfully assaulted Burnside's Bridge. Then the brigade suffered heavy casualties at Fredericksburg in December.[2]

Nagle's appointment as brigadier general of volunteers expired without confirmation on March 4, 1863, but he was soon reappointed to rank from March 13. He continued to lead his brigade that spring after it was sent to the Army of the Ohio, but poor health caused him to resign on May 9, 1863. The next month he organized the 39th Pennsylvania Militia, a ninety-day regiment raised in response to the Confederate invasion of Pennsylvania. On July 1 he was named the regiment's colonel and the regiment was mustered out on August 2, 1863 after seeing no combat.[3]

On July 24, 1864, Nagle was named colonel of the 194th Pennsylvania, a 100-day militia regiment he raised and organized in response to Jubal Early's Washington, D.C. raid. The regiment mustered out on November 5, 1864, after guarding the approaches to Baltimore. Thus Nagle had the distinction of commanding four different Pennsylvania regiments during the war. He died two years later in Pottsville.[4]

Presbyterian Cemetery is located on West Howard Avenue, between 11th and 12th Streets, near downtown Pottsville. The cemetery is on a steep hill and there are no roads in the cemetery. Nagle's grave is approximately in the center of the cemetery.

92

READING

CHARLES EVANS CEMETERY

DAVID McMURTRIE GREGG

Born: April 10, 1833
Died: August 7, 1916

General Gregg was born in Huntingdon, Pennsylvania. His cousin, Andrew Gregg Curtain, served as governor of Pennsylvania during the Civil War. Gregg received his education at local private schools and at the University of Lewisburg (now Bucknell University). He graduated from West Point in 1855, ranked 8th out of 34, and he was appointed second lieutenant in the dragoons on September 4, 1855. He served on the western frontier and in California until the Civil War, and he was promoted to first lieutenant on March 21, 1861.[1]

On May 14, 1861, Gregg was named captain in the 3rd U.S. Cavalry. On August 3, 1861, he was transferred to the 6th U.S. Cavalry, and then he was appointed colonel of the 8th Pennsylvania Cavalry on January 24, 1862. He ably led this regiment in action during the Peninsula Campaign of 1862 and he was commissioned brigadier general of volunteers as of November 29, 1862. He then commanded a brigade of cavalry during the Fredericksburg Campaign. He led a cavalry division at Chancellorsville and at Gettysburg. At the latter battle his division guarded the Union right flank and it repulsed Jeb Stuart's Confederate cavalry in a clash on July 3.[2]

During the Overland Campaign of 1864 Gregg continued to lead his division, gaining a reputation for conspicuous leadership and gallantry. He was brevetted to major general of volunteers on August 1, 1864, but he unexpectedly resigned from the army on

February 3, 1865. In his resignation letter Gregg merely stated that pressing personal matters at home necessitated his abrupt resignation.[3]

At first Gregg lived in Reading, Pennsylvania, the home of his second wife. Then Gregg took up farming and fruit growing near Milford, Delaware. In 1874 he was appointed U.S. Consul at Prague, but he resigned the post in August of that year, because his wife was homesick, and returned to Reading. He wrote a book on his cavalry division's performance during the Gettysburg Campaign and he was active in local and charitable affairs. He died in Reading.[4]

READING

CHARLES EVANS CEMETERY

WILLIAM HIGH KEIM

Born: June 25, 1813
Died: May 18, 1862

General Keim was born near Reading, Pennsylvania. He was educated at Mt. Airy Military Academy and he was very active in local militias for many years prior to the Civil War. In 1848 Keim was elected mayor of Reading, and he served as a U.S. Representative from Pennsylvania from December 7, 1858, until March 3, 1859, filling a vacancy. He became Surveyor General of Pennsylvania in 1860 and he held that position until his death.[1]

Keim was commissioned major general of the Pennsylvania militia on April 20, 1861. The militia was sent to the Shenandoah Valley under the command of General Robert Patterson, although it was not mustered into the Federal service. Keim served as a division commander and as the second in command under Patterson. The militia and Keim were mustered out on July 21, 1861, after Patterson's failure to keep Joseph Johnston's command from reinforcing the Confederate forces at Manassas during the First Manassas Campaign.[2]

Evidently Keim was not blamed for Patterson's shortcomings, for on December 20, 1861, Keim was commissioned brigadier general of volunteers. He commanded a brigade in the 4th Corps of the Army of the Potomac at the beginning of the Peninsula Campaign in the spring of 1862, but in early May he contracted a fever (possibly typhoid fever). During the fighting at Williamsburg on May 5, 1862, he was barely able to remain on his horse because of his illness. He returned to Pennsylvania to try to recover from his ailment, arriving in Harrisburg on May 14, but he died there four days later.[3]

READING

CHARLES EVANS CEMETERY

ALEXANDER SCHIMMELFENNIG

Born: July 20, 1824
Died: September 5, 1865

General Schimmelfennig was born in Lithauen, Prussia. He served in the Prussian Army, being an ensign in 1840 and a lieutenant in 1842. As noted on his grave marker, "he resigned his commission to sustain the republican cause on the battle fields of Schleswig Holstein, the Palatinate, and Baden." When his revolutionary cause was defeated, he fled to Switzerland. In 1853 he moved to the United States and he took up residence in Philadelphia, where he worked as a draftsman and an engineer. It is possible that by 1860 he was in Washington, D.C. working as a draftsman and engineer for the War Department.[1]

On September 30, 1861, Schimmelfennig was commissioned colonel of the 74th Pennsylvania. While the regiment was marching in the streets of Philadelphia, on its way to Washington, D.C., his horse fell and Schimmelfennig severely injured his ankle. He stayed behind to recuperate, but he then contracted smallpox. He briefly rejoined his regiment several weeks later, but the ankle injury became aggravated and he had to take sick leave until the next summer. On August 22, 1862, upon the death of General Henry Bohlen, Schimmelfennig was given command of Bohlen's brigade in the Army of Virginia. He led the brigade during the Second Manassas Campaign, and then on September 12, 1862, he was given command of an 11th Corps brigade in the Army of the Potomac. On November 29, 1862, he was commissioned brigadier general of volunteers.[2]

Schimmelfennig's brigade was among the 11th Corps forces routed on the evening of May 2, 1863, by Stonewall Jackson's Confederates at Chancellorsville, although blame for this disaster rested with his superiors. Then on July 1, 1863, during the first day of the Battle of Gettysburg, he had temporary command of his division. When his division was forced to retreat, Schimmelfennig was wounded and cut off from his troops, but he was able to hide in a pigsty (or stable or woodshed) in the town of Gettysburg during the remainder of the battle. When the Confederates evacuated the town, he was able to rejoin his unit safely.[3]

Schimmelfennig requested a transfer after the 11th Corps became the object of scorn for its poor showing at both Chancellorsville and Gettysburg and in August 1863 he was transferred to South Carolina. From August 16, 1863, until April 1865, he commanded several different brigades and divisions, and a district, in the Department of the South, although he was on sick leave, suffering from malaria or dysentery, from November 1863 until February 1864. He was placed in command of Charleston, South Carolina, in February 1865 after that city's fall to Union forces, but on April 8, 1865, he took sick leave after contracting tuberculosis. He went back to Pennsylvania, searching for relief from his illness, but he died near Wernersville, Pennsylvania on September 5, 1865.[4]

Charles Evans Cemetery is located at 1119 Centre Avenue in downtown Reading. Gregg's grave is number 15 on the map (located behind the distinctive Charles Evans grave marker), Keim's grave is number 3 on the map, and Schimmelfennig's grave is number 28 on the map.

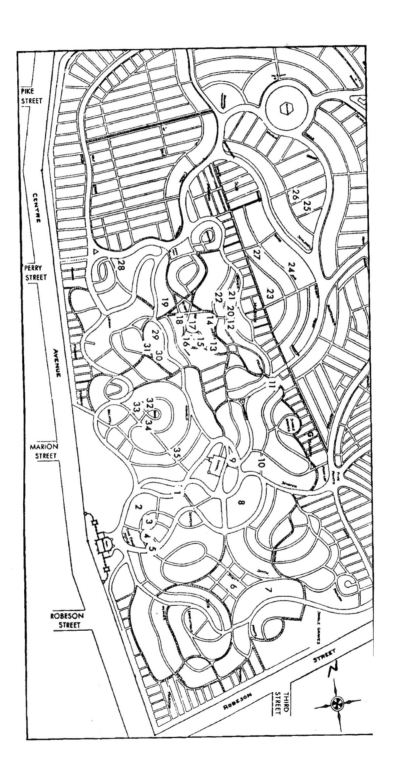

YORK

PROSPECT HILL CEMETERY

WILLIAM BUEL FRANKLIN

Born: February 27, 1823
Died: March 8, 1903

General Franklin was born in York, Pennsylvania, and he graduated from West Point in 1843, ranked 1st out of 39. He then joined the elite Corps of Topographical Engineers and he participated in both the 1843-1845 Great Lakes survey and the Rocky Mountains expedition of Philip Kearny. On September 21, 1846, he was promoted to second lieutenant and he served in the Mexican War, earning a brevet to first lieutenant for his gallantry at Buena Vista. From the end of that war until the Civil War he held a variety of positions, including instructor at West Point, supervisor of harbor improvements, and director of the construction of the Capitol Building dome and the Treasury addition in Washington, D.C. He was promoted to first lieutenant in 1853 and to captain in 1857.[1]

On May 14, 1861, Franklin was named colonel of the 12th U.S. Infantry and on May 17, 1861, he was commissioned brigadier general of volunteers. At First Manassas he commanded a brigade and on October 3, 1861, he was given command of a division in the Army of the Potomac. At the beginning of the Peninsula Campaign he commanded a 1st Corps division, but on May 18, 1862, he was placed in command of the 6th Corps, which he commanded throughout the Seven Days Battles and during the Antietam Campaign. On July 4, 1862, Franklin was promoted to major general of volunteers.[2]

When General Ambrose Burnside took command of the Army of the Potomac in November 1862 he divided the army into three large Grand Divisions, and Franklin was given command of the Left Grand Division on November 16, 1862. At Fredericksburg on December 13 Franklin's forces temporarily penetrated the Confederate right, but a lack of support caused the Union attack to fail. Although this constituted the only bright spot for the Union in this disastrous battle, Burnside complained that Franklin was partially responsible for the Union defeat and he demanded that Franklin be removed from the army. President Abraham Lincoln refused to cashier Franklin from the army. On July 28, 1863, Franklin was reassigned to the Department of the Gulf, where he was briefly in command of a division in the 19th Corps until August 20. On that date Franklin was given command of the 19th Corps, which he led in the Sabine Pass and Red River Campaigns. During the latter campaign he was wounded in the leg at Mansfield, Louisiana.[3]

While on sick leave to recover from his wound, Franklin was captured by Jubal Early's Confederates near Washington, D.C. on July 11, 1864, but he was able to escape the next night. He spent the rest of the war serving on boards and awaiting further orders that never came. On March 13, 1865, he received a brevet promotion to major general in the Regular Army. On March 15, 1866, he resigned from the army.[4]

After the war Franklin moved to Connecticut and he was involved in a variety of ventures. He was the general manager of the Colt's Fire Arms Manufacturing Company for 22 years, the supervisor of the construction of the Connecticut Capitol, a presidential elector for Democrat Samuel Tilden in 1876, and the Commissioner General of the United States for the Paris Exposition of 1888. He died in Hartford, Connecticut.[5]

Prospect Hill Cemetery is located at 700 N. George Street, in the northern part of downtown York. Franklin's grave is in Section H, near the road in the cemetery, as marked on the map.

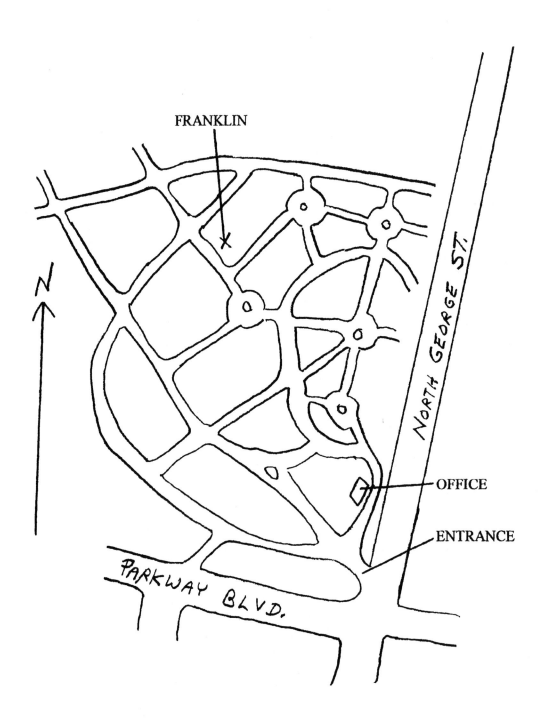

ENDNOTES

ABBREVIATIONS

The following abbreviations are used in the notes for these frequently cited sources.

APWH

Blake A. Magner, *At Peace with Honor: The Civil War Burials of Laurel Hill Cemetery, Philadelphia, Pennsylvania* (Collingswood, NJ: C.W. Historicals, 1997)

CWD

Mark M. Boatner III, *The Civil War Dictionary* (New York: David McKay Company, Inc., 1959)

CWG

James Spencer, compiler, *Civil War Generals: Categorical Listings and Biographical Directory* (New York: Greenwood Press, 1986)

CWHC

John H. Eicher and David J. Eicher, *Civil War High Commands* (Stanford, CA: Stanford University Press, 2001)

GG

Larry Tagg, *The Generals of Gettysburg: The Leaders of America's Greatest Battle* (Campbell, CA: Savas Publishing Company, 1998)

GIB

Ezra J. Warner, *Generals in Blue: Lives of the Union Commanders* (Baton Rouge, LA: Louisiana State University Press, 1964)

HTIE

Patricia L. Faust, editor, *Historical Times Illustrated Encyclopedia of the Civil War* (New York: Harper & Row, 1986)

MHUG

Jack D. Welsh, *Medical Histories of Union Generals* (Kent, OH: The Kent State University Press, 1996)

OR

United States War Department, *The War of the Rebellion: A Compilation of the Official Records of the Union and Confederate Armies*, 70 vols. in 128 parts (Washington, D.C.: U.S. Government Printing Office, 1880-1901)

Herman Haupt

1. *GIB*, p. 217; *MHUG*, p. 160; *CWD*, p. 386; *HTIE*, p. 351; *CWHC*, p. 287; Francis A. Lord, *Lincoln's Railroad Man: Herman Haupt* (Rutherford, NJ: Fairleigh Dickinson University Press, 1969), pp. 21-31; James A. Ward, *That Man Haupt: A Biography of Herman Haupt* (Baton Rouge, LA: Louisiana State University Press, 1973), pp. 5-104.

2. *GIB*, pp. 217-218; *MHUG*, p. 160; *CWD*, p. 386; *HTIE*, p. 351; *CWHC*, p. 287; Lord, pp. 31-257; Ward, pp. 104-170.

3. *GIB*, p. 218; *MHUG*, p. 160; *CWD*, p. 386; *HTIE*, p. 351; *CWHC*, p. 287; Lord, pp. 258-291; Ward, pp. 171-250.

William Reading Montgomery

1. *GIB*, pp. 329-330; *MHUG*, p. 234; *CWD*, p. 562; *CWHC*, p. 394.

2. *GIB*, p. 330; *MHUG*, p. 234; *CWD*, p. 562; *CWHC*, p. 394.

3. *GIB*, p. 330; *MHUG*, p. 234.

Thomas Welsh

1. *GIB*, p. 550; *MHUG*, p. 364; *CWHC*, p. 560; *CWG*, pp. 80, 299. All four of these sources give May 5, 1824, as Welsh's date of birth; however, his grave marker gives May 3, 1824, as the date.

2. *GIB*, p. 550; *MHUG*, p. 364; *CWD*, p. 901; *CWHC*, p. 560.

3. *GIB*, pp. 550-551; *MHUG*, p. 364; *CWD*, p. 901; *CWHC*, p. 560; *CWG*, pp. 176, 299. Boatner gives August 18, 1863, as Welsh's date of death; however, Warner, Welsh, Eicher, Spencer, and Welsh's grave marker all give August 14, 1863, as the date of death.

Charles Adam Heckman

1. *GIB*, pp. 226-227; *MHUG*, p. 166; *HTIE*, p. 356; *CWHC*, p. 292.

2. *GIB*, p. 227; *MHUG*, p. 166; *CWD*, p. 391; *HTIE*, p. 356; *CWHC*, p. 292.

3. *GIB*, p. 227; *MHUG*, p. 166; *CWD*, p. 392; *HTIE*, p. 356; *CWHC*, p. 292; *OR*, Series 1, vol. 42, pt. 1, pp. 793-795; *OR*, Series 2, vol. 7, p. 805.

4. *GIB*, p. 227; *MHUG*, p. 166; *CWD*, p. 392; *HTIE*, p. 356; *CWHC*, p. 292; *CWG*, pp. 187, 254. Welsh gives January 15, 1896, as Heckman's date of death; however, Warner, Faust, Eicher, and Spencer give January 14, 1896, as the date.

Strong Vincent

1. *GIB*, p. 527; *MHUG*, p. 353; *CWD*, p. 878; *HTIE*, p. 786; *GG*, p. 90; *CWHC*, p. 614; James H. Nevins and William B. Styple, *What Death More Glorious: A Biography of General Strong Vincent* (Kearny, NJ: Belle Grove Publishing Co., 1997), pp. 11-27.

2. *GIB*, pp. 527-528; *MHUG*, p. 353; *CWD*, p. 878; *HTIE*, p. 786; *GG*, p. 90; *CWHC*, p. 614; Nevins and Styple, pp. 31-59.

3. *GIB*, p. 528; *MHUG*, p. 353; *CWD*, p. 878; *HTIE*, p. 786; *GG*, p. 90; *CWHC*, p. 614; Nevins and Styple, pp. 67-89.

John White Geary

1. *GIB*, p. 169; *MHUG*, p. 127; *CWD*, p. 327; *HTIE*, p. 302; *GG*, p. 155; *CWHC*, p. 251; William Alan Blair, editor, *A Politician Goes To War: The Civil War Letters of John White Geary* (University Park, PA: The Pennsylvania State University Press, 1995), pp. ix-x, xvii-xviii.

2. *GIB*, pp. 169-170; *MHUG*, pp. 127-128; *CWD*, pp. 327-328; *HTIE*, p. 302; *GG*, pp. 155-156; *CWHC*, pp. 251-252; Blair, pp. xviii-xix. Boatner, Tagg, and Eicher all state that Geary was captured in March 1862 and then exchanged, but there is no reference to his capture or exchange in the *Official Records* or in Geary's letters found in Blair. Also, Warner, Welsh, and Faust make no mention of his capture or exchange. Warner does state that Geary captured the town of Leesburg, Virginia, in March 1862. I surmise that Boatner, Tagg, and Eicher misconstrued this statement by Warner and so they incorrectly reported that Geary himself was captured at that time. This belief is reinforced by the fact that both Boatner and Eicher state that Geary was captured at Leesburg, the town that Geary captured.

3. *GIB*, p. 170; *MHUG*, p. 128; *CWD*, p. 328; *HTIE*, p. 302; *GG*, p. 157; *CWHC*, p. 252; Blair, pp. xx-xxii.

4. *GIB*, p. 170; *MHUG*, p. 128; *CWD*, p. 328; *HTIE*, p. 302; *GG*, p. 157; *CWHC*, p. 252; *CWG*, pp. 179, 246; Blair, p. xviii. Welsh and Spencer give January 18, 1873, as Geary's date of death and Eicher gives February 18, 1873, as the date of death; however, Faust, Blair, and Geary's grave marker all give February 8, 1873, as the date.

Joseph Farmer Knipe

1. *GIB*, p. 272; *CWD*, p. 466; *CWHC*, p. 336.

2. *GIB*, p. 272; *MHUG*, pp. 196-197; *CWD*, p. 466; *CWHC*, p. 336.

3. *GIB*, p. 272; *MHUG*, p. 197; *CWD*, p. 466; *CWHC*, p. 336.

4. *GIB*, p. 272; *MHUG*, p. 197; *CWD*, p. 466; *CWHC*, p. 336.

LaFayette Curry Baker

1. *GIB*, pp. 16-17; *CWD*, p. 39; *HTIE*, p. 34; *CWHC*, p. 588.

2. *GIB*, p. 17; *CWD*, p. 39; *HTIE*, p. 34.

3. *GIB*, p. 17; *CWD*, p. 39; *HTIE*, pp. 34-35.

4. *GIB*, p. 17; *MHUG*, p. 14; *CWD*, pp. 39-40; *HTIE*, p. 35; *CWHC*, p. 588.

5. *GIB*, p. 17; *HTIE*, p. 35.

6. *GIB*, p. 17.

Thomas Leiper Kane

1. *GIB*, p. 256; *CWD*, p. 447; *GG*, p. 159; *APWH*, p. 65.

2. *GIB*, pp. 256-257; *CWD*, p. 447; *GG*, pp. 159-160; *APWH*, p. 65.

3. *GIB*, p. 257; *MHUG*, p. 186; *CWD*, p. 447; *GG*, p. 160; *CWHC*, p. 327; *APWH*, p. 65; *OR*, Series 2, vol. 4, pp. 400, 438.

4. *GIB*, p. 257; *MHUG*, pp. 186-187; *CWD*, p. 447; *GG*, pp. 160-161; *CWHC*, p. 327; *APWH*, p. 65.

5. *GIB*, p. 257; *MHUG*, p. 187; *GG*, p. 161; *CWHC*, p. 327; *APWH*, p. 65.

John Fulton Reynolds

1. *GIB*, p. 396; *MHUG*, p. 275; *HTIE* p. 625; *CWHC*, p. 451; *CWG*, pp. 77, 280. All five of these sources give September 20, 1820, as Reynolds' date of birth, however, his grave marker gives September 21, 1820, as the date.

2. *GIB*, p. 396; *MHUG*, p. 275; *CWD*, p. 694; *HTIE*, pp. 625-626; *GG*, p. 10; Edward J. Nichols, *Toward Gettysburg: A Biography of General John F. Reynolds* (University Park, PA: The Pennsylvania State University Press, 1958), pp. 3-74.

3. *GIB*, pp. 396-397; *MHUG*, p. 275; *CWD*, p. 694; *HTIE*, p. 626; *GG*, p. 10; Nichols, pp. 74-100.

4. *GIB*, p. 397; *HTIE*, p. 626; *CWD*, p. 694; *GG*, pp. 9-11; Nichols, pp. 100-184, 220-223.

5. *GIB*, p. 397; *MHUG*, p. 275; *CWD*, p. 694; *HTIE*, p. 626; *GG*, pp. 11-12; Nichols, pp. 184-205.

Charles Henry Van Wyck

1. *GIB*, pp. 524-525; *MHUG*, p. 351.

2. *GIB*, p. 525; *MHUG*, p. 351; *CWD*, p. 868.

3. *GIB*, p. 525; *MHUG*, p. 351; *CWD*, p. 868.

Winfield Scott Hancock

1. *GIB*, pp. 202-203; *MHUG*, p. 149; *CWD*, p. 372; *HTIE*, p. 337; *GG*, p. 33; *CWHC*, p. 277; Glenn Tucker, *Hancock The Superb* (Dayton, OH: Morningside Bookshop (Reprint), 1980), pp. 18-66; David M. Jordan, *Winfield Scott Hancock: A Soldier's Life* (Bloomington , IN: Indiana University Press, 1988), pp. 5-34.

2. *GIB*, p. 203; *MHUG*, pp. 149-150; *CWD*, p. 372; *HTIE*, p. 337; *GG*, pp. 33-34; *CWHC*, pp. 277-278; Tucker, pp. 66-124; Jordan, pp. 35-74.

3. *GIB*, p. 203; *MHUG*, p. 150; *HTIE*, p. 337; *GG*, pp. 34-35; *CWHC*, p. 278; Tucker, pp. 125-164; Jordan, pp. 75-100.

4. *GIB*, p. 203-204; *MHUG*, p. 150; *CWD*, p. 372; *HTIE*, p. 337; Tucker, pp. 177-266; Jordan, pp. 110-175.

5. *GIB*, p. 204; *MHUG*, pp. 150-151; *CWD*, p. 372; *HTIE*, pp. 337-338; *GG*, p. 35; Tucker, pp. 266-311; Jordan, pp. 176-315.

John Frederick Hartranft

1. *GIB* p. 211; *MHUG*, p. 155; *HTIE*, p. 347; *CWHC*, p. 284.

2. *GIB*, pp. 211-212; *MHUG*, p. 155; *HTIE*, p. 347; *CWHC*, p. 284.

3. *GIB*, p. 212; *MHUG*, p. 155; *CWD*, p. 382; *HTIE*, pp. 347-348; *CWHC*, p. 284.

4. *GIB*, p. 212; *MHUG*, p. 155; *CWD*, p. 382; *HTIE*, p. 348; *CWHC*, p. 284.

Adam Jacoby Slemmer

1. *GIB*, p. 450; *MHUG*, p. 305; *CWD*, p. 764; *CWHC*, p. 491; *CWG*, pp. 84, 286. Boatner gives 1828 as the year of Slemmer's birth, however, Warner, Welsh, Eicher, Spencer, and Slemmer's grave marker all give 1829 as the year.

2. *GIB*, p. 450; *MHUG*, p. 305; *CWD*, p. 764; *CWHC*, p. 491.

3. *GIB*, pp. 450-451; *MHUG*, p. 305; *CWD*, p. 764; *CWHC*, p. 491.

4. *GIB*, p. 451; *MHUG*, p. 305; *CWD*, p. 765. Eicher states (*CWHC*, p. 491) that Slemmer was an assistant inspector general for the Army of the Ohio from March until October of 1862, but there is no mention of this in the *Official Records*. Welsh states that Slemmer returned to command of his regiment in May 1862, Warner states that Slemmer served under General Don C. Buell in 1862 in his (Buell's) operations in Mississippi, northern Alabama, Tennessee, and Kentucky, and Boatner states that Slemmer served with Buell from May until November 1862. In the *Official Records* Slemmer is listed as commander of the 16th U.S. Infantry on both June 10 and October 8 of 1862. *OR*, Series 1, vol. 16, pt. 2, pp. 5, 591.

5. *GIB*, p. 451; *MHUG*, p. 305; *CWD*, p. 765.

Samuel Kosciuszko Zook

1. *GIB*, p. 576; *MHUG*, p. 380; *CWD*, p. 954; *GG*, p. 40; *CWHC*, p. 586; *CWG*, pp. 78, 303. Boatner gives 1823 as the year of Zook's birth, however, Warner, Welsh, Spencer, and Eicher give 1821 as the year. Tagg states that Zook was 42 at the start of the Gettysburg Campaign, which would make his year of birth 1821. Zook's grave marker states he was 41 when he died, which would make his year of birth 1822.

2. *GIB,* p. 576; *MHUG*, p. 380; *CWD*, p. 954; *GG*, pp. 40-41; *CWHC*, p. 586.

3. *GIB*, pp. 576-577; *MHUG*, p. 380; *CWD*, p. 954; *GG*, p. 41; *CWHC*, p. 587.

4. *GIB*, p. 577; *MHUG*, p. 380; *CWD*, p. 954; *GG*, pp. 41-42; *CWHC*, p. 587.

George Cadwalader

1. *GIB*, p. 63; *MHUG*, p. 51; *CWD*, p. 112; *CWHC*, p. 158; *CWG*, pp. 72, 230. Boatner gives 1803 as the year of Cadwalader's birth, however, Warner, Welsh, Eicher, Spencer, and Cadwalader's grave marker all give 1806 as the year.

2. *GIB,* p. 63*; MHUG*, p. 51; *CWD*, p. 112; *CWHC*, p. 158.

3. *GIB*, p. 63; *CWD*, p. 112; *CWHC*, p. 158.

4. *GIB*, p. 63; *CWD*, p. 112; *MHUG*, p. 51; *CWHC*, p. 158; Michael A. Cavanaugh, Introduction, *Military Essays and Recollections of the Pennsylvania Commandery, Military Order of the Loyal Legion of the United States* (Wilmington, NC: Broadfoot Publishing Company (Reprint), 1995), vol. 1, pp. iii-iv.

George Archibald McCall

1. *GIB*, p. 289; *MHUG*, pp. 208-209; *CWD*, pp. 522-523; *CWHC*, p. 370.

2. *GIB*, pp. 289-290; *MHUG*, p. 209; *CWD*, p. 523; *CWHC*, p. 370.

3. *GIB*, p. 290; *MHUG*, p. 209; *CWD*, p. 523; *CWHC*, p. 370; *CWG*, pp. 178, 267. Warner and Spencer give February 26, 1868, as General McCall's date of death.

Welsh and Eicher give February 25, 1868, as the date of death. Boatner gives 1868 as the year of McCall's death. But McCall's grave marker gives February 25, 1867, as the date of death.

William Henry Charles Bohlen

1. *GIB*, p. 38; *MHUG*, p. 33; *CWD*, p. 72; *APWH*, p. 3; *CWHC*, p. 136; *CWG*, p. 227. Warner, Welsh, Boatner, Spencer, and the *Official Records* all refer to General Bohlen as "Henry Bohlen," however, Magner and Eicher refer to him as "William Henry Charles Bohlen." His grave marker gives his name as "W. Henry C. Bohlen." Thus it seems that although his name was "William Henry Charles," he was known by the name "Henry."

2. *GIB*, pp. 38-39; *MHUG*, p. 33; *CWD*, p. 72; *APWH*, pp. 3-4; *CWHC*, p. 136.

3. *GIB*, p. 39; *CWD*, p. 72; *APWH*, p. 4; *CWHC*, p. 136. An excellent account of the ill-fated reconnaissance at Freeman's Ford is found in John J. Hennessy, *Return to Bull Run: The Campaign and Battle of Second Manassas* (New York: Simon & Schuster, 1993), pp. 68-70.

Samuel Wylie Crawford

1. *GIB*, p. 99; *MHUG*, p. 80; *CWD*, p. 207; *HTIE*, p. 191; *APWH*, p. 7; *GG*, p. 97; *CWHC*, p. 190; *CWG*, pp. 84, 236. Warner, Boatner, Faust, Magner, Eicher, and Spencer all give 1829 as the year of Crawford's birth, however, Welsh and Crawford's grave marker both give 1827 as the year of his birth. Welsh states that when Crawford applied for retirement Crawford reported that he had been born in 1827. This date makes more sense, considering the fact that Crawford graduated from college in 1846. Tagg states that Crawford was 44 at the time of Gettysburg, which would make his year of birth 1828.

2. *GIB*, p. 99; *MHUG*, p. 80; *CWD*, p. 207; *HTIE*, p. 191; *APWH*, p. 7; *GG*, p. 98; *CWHC*, p. 190.

3. *GIB*, p. 99; *MHUG*, pp. 80-81; *CWD*, p. 207; *HTIE*, p. 191; *APWH*, pp. 7-8; *GG*, p. 98; *CWHC*, p. 190.

4. *GIB*, pp. 99-100; *MHUG*, pp. 81-82; *CWD*, pp. 207-208; *HTIE*, p. 191; *APWH*, p. 8; *GG*, p. 99; *CWHC*, p. 190.

George Gordon Meade

1. *GIB*, p. 315; *HTIE*, p. 482; *GG*, p. 1; *APWH*, p. 28; Freeman Cleaves, *Meade of Gettysburg* (Dayton, OH: Morningside Bookshop (Reprint), 1980), pp. 3-9. Meade's father was released from prison in 1818, but he died ten years later at the age of 50.

2. *GIB*, pp. 315-316; *MHUG*, pp. 224-225; *CWD*, p. 539; *HTIE*, p. 482; *APWH*, p. 28; *CWHC*, p. 384; Cleaves, pp. 9-15.

3. *GIB*, p. 316; *CWD*, p. 539; *HTIE*, p. 482; *APWH*, pp. 28-29; *CWHC*, pp. 384-385; Cleaves, pp. 15-54.

4. *GIB*, p. 316; *MHUG*, p. 225; *HTIE*, p. 482; *GG*, p. 2; *APWH*, p. 29; *CWHC*, p. 385; Cleaves, pp. 55-69.

5. *GIB*, p. 316; *MHUG*, p. 225; *HTIE*, p. 482; *GG*, pp. 2-3; *APWH*, p. 29; *CWHC*, p. 385; Cleaves, pp. 72-93.

6. *GIB*, p. 316; *HTIE*, p. 482; *GG*, pp. 1-7; *APWH*, pp. 29-30; *CWHC*, p. 385; Cleaves, pp. 95-183.

7. *GIB*, p. 317; *HTIE*, p. 482; *APWH*, p. 30; *CWHC*, p. 385; Cleaves, pp. 184-333.

8. *GIB*, p. 317; *MHUG*, pp. 225-226; *CWD*, pp. 539-540; *HTIE*, pp. 482-483; *APWH*, p. 30; Cleaves, pp. 334-352. Magner states that Meade died on November 7, 1872, however, all of the other cited sources, as well as Meade's grave marker, give November 6, 1872 as the date of death.

James St. Clair Morton

1. *GIB*, p. 336; *MHUG*, p. 237; *CWD*, p. 570; *HTIE*, p. 512; *APWH*, p. 33; *CWHC*, p. 400.

2. *GIB*, p. 336; *MHUG*, p. 237; *CWD*, p. 570; *HTIE*, pp. 512-513; *APWH*, pp. 33-34; *CWHC*, p. 400.

3. *GIB*, p. 336; *MHUG*, p. 237; *CWD*, p. 570; *HTIE*, p. 513; *APWH*, p. 34; *CWHC*, p. 400.

Henry Morris Naglee

1. *GIB*, p. 340; *MHUG*, p. 239; *APWH*, p. 35; *CWHC*, p. 403; *CWG*, pp. 74, 272. All five of these sources give January 15, 1815, as Naglee's date of birth, however, his grave marker gives January 14, 1815, as the date.

2. *GIB*, pp. 340-341; *MHUG*, p. 239; *CWD*, p. 578; *APWH*, p. 35; *CWHC*, p. 403.

3. *GIB*, p. 341; *MHUG*, p. 239; *CWD*, p. 578; *APWH*, p. 35; *CWHC*, p. 403.

4. *GIB*, p. 341; *MHUG*, p. 239; *CWD*, p. 578; *APWH*, p. 35; *CWHC*, p. 403.

5. *GIB*, p. 341; *MHUG*, p. 239; *CWD*, p. 578; *APWH*, p. 35; *CWHC*, p. 403.

Joshua Thomas Owen

1. *GIB*, p. 353; *MHUG*, p. 247; *CWD*, p. 614; *APWH*, p. 36; *CWHC*, p. 412.

2. *GIB*, pp. 353-354; *MHUG*, pp. 247-248; *CWD*, p. 614; *APWH*, p. 36; *CWHC*, p. 412.

3. *GIB*, p. 354; *MHUG*, p. 248; *CWD*, p. 614; *APWH*, pp. 36-37; *CWHC*, p. 412.

4. *GIB*, p. 354; *MHUG*, p. 248; *APWH*, p. 37; *CWHC*, p. 412.

Francis Engle Patterson

1. *GIB*, p. 362; *MHUG*, p. 253; *CWD*, p. 623; *APWH*, p. 38; *CWHC*, p. 418; *CWG*, pp. 78, 274. Boatner gives 1827 as the year of Patterson's birth, however, all of the other listed sources, as well as Patterson's grave marker, give May 7, 1821, as his birth date. Warner's footnote number 460 (*GIB*, p. 649) states that published sources had usually given June 24, 1827, as Patterson's birth date, but that Patterson's tombstone inscription and his contemporaneous death notices all listed May 7, 1821, as the date of birth.

2. *GIB*, pp. 362-363; *CWD*, p. 623; *APWH*, pp. 38-39; *CWHC*, p. 418.

3. *GIB*, p. 363; *MHUG* p. 253; *CWD*, p. 623; *APWH*, p. 39; *CWHC*, p. 418.

4. *GIB*, p. 363; *MHUG*, p. 253; *CWD*, p. 623; *APWH*, p. 39; *CWHC*, p. 418; *OR*, Series 1, vol. 19, pt. 2, pp. 562-563.

John Clifford Pemberton

1. Ezra J. Warner, *Generals In Gray: Lives of the Confederate Commanders* (Baton Rouge, LA: Louisiana State University Press, 1959), p. 232; Jack D. Welsh, *Medical Histories of Confederate Generals* (Kent, OH: The Kent State University Press, 1995), p. 166; *CWD*, p. 631; *HTIE*, p. 569; *APWH*, pp. 42-43; *CWHC*, p. 423; Michael B. Ballard, *Pemberton: A Biography* (Jackson, MS: University Press of Mississippi, 1991), pp. 5-82.

2. Warner, p. 232; Welsh, p. 166; *CWD*, p. 631; *HTIE*, p. 569; *APWH*, p. 43; Ballard, pp. 83-86.

3. Warner, pp. 232-233; Welsh, p. 166; *CWD*, p. 631; *HTIE*, p. 569; *APWH*, p. 43; *CWHC*, p. 423; Ballard, pp. 86-180.

4. Warner, p. 233; *CWD*, p. 631; *HTIE*, p. 569; Ballard, pp. 180-185.

5. Warner, p. 233; Welsh, p. 166; *CWD*, p. 631; *HTIE*, p. 569; Ballard, pp. 185-202.

Charles Ferguson Smith

1. *GIB*, p. 455; *MHUG*, p. 308; *CWD*, p. 769; *HTIE*, p. 694; *APWH*, pp. 51-52; *CWHC*, p. 493.

2. *GIB*, p. 455; *CWD*, p. 769; *HTIE*, pp. 694-695; *APWH*, p. 52; *CWHC*, p. 493.

3. *GIB*, p. 455; *CWD*, p. 769; *HTIE*, p. 695; *APWH*, p. 52; *CWHC*, p. 493.

4. *GIB*, pp. 455-456; *MHUG*, p. 308; *CWD*, p. 769; *HTIE*, p. 695; *APWH*, p. 52; *CWHC*, p. 493.

Alfred Sully

1. *GIB*, p. 488; *MHUG*, p. 327; *CWD*, p. 818; *APWH*, p. 53; *CWHC*, p. 518; *CWG*, pp. 77, 291. Warner, Welsh, Magner, Eicher, and Spencer all give 1820 as the year of Sully's birth, however, Boatner gives 1821 as the year of birth. The title of General Sully's biography, *No Tears for the General*, by Langdon Sully, gives 1821 as the year of his birth.

2. *GIB*, p. 488; *MHUG*, p. 327; *CWD*, p. 818; *APWH*, p. 53; *CWHC*, p. 518; Langdon Sully, *No Tears for the General: The Life of Alfred Sully, 1821-1879* (Palo Alto, CA: American West Publishing Co., 1974), pp. 9-10, 17-1427

3. *GIB*, pp. 488-489; *MHUG*, pp. 327-328; *CWD*, p. 818; *APWH*, pp. 53-54; *CWHC*, p. 518; Sully, pp. 128-214.

4. *GIB*, p. 489; *MHUG*, p. 328; *CWD*, p. 818; *APWH*, p. 54; *CWHC*, p. 518; Sully, pp. 214-233.

Hector Tyndale

1. According to Warner, Tyndale's death certificate indicates that his full name was George Hector Tyndale. *GIB*, p. 516. Welsh and Spencer both list him as George Hector Tyndale. *MHUG*, p. 345; *CWG*, p. 295. Eicher lists him as (George) Hector Tyndale. *CWHC*, p. 539. Boatner, Faust, Magner, and Tyndale's grave marker all list him as merely Hector Tyndale. *CWD*, p. 856; *HTIE*, p. 768; *APWH*, p. 55.

2. *GIB*, pp. 516-517; *CWD*, p. 856; *HTIE*, p. 768; *APWH*, pp. 55-56.

3. *GIB*, p. 517; *MHUG*, pp. 345-346; *CWD*, p. 856; *HTIE*, p. 769; *APWH*, p. 56; *CWHC*, p. 539.

4. *GIB*, p. 517; *MHUG*, p. 346; *CWD*, p. 856; *HTIE*, p. 769; *APWH*, p. 56.

5. *GIB*, p. 517; *HTIE*, p. 769; *APWH*, p. 56.

Galusha Pennypacker

1. *GIB*, p. 365; *HTIE*, p. 574.

2. *GIB*, pp. 365-366; *MHUG*, p. 254; *CWD*, p. 640; *HTIE*, p. 574; *CWHC*, p. 425.

3. *GIB*, p. 366; *MHUG*, p.255; *CWD*, p. 640; *HTIE*, p. 574; *CWHC*, p. 425.

4. *GIB*, p. 366; *MHUG*, p. 255; *CWD*, p. 640; *HTIE*, p. 574; *CWHC*, p. 425.

5. *GIB*, p. 366; *MHUG*, p. 255; *CWD*, p. 640; *HTIE*, p. 574; *CWHC*, p. 425.

Thomas Kilby Smith

1. *GIB*, pp. 461-462; *MHUG*, p. 312; *CWD*, p. 774; *CWHC*, p. 499.

2. *GIB*, p. 462; *MHUG*, p. 312; *CWD*, p. 774; *CWHC*, p. 499.

3. *GIB*, p. 462; *MHUG*, pp. 312-313; *CWD*, p. 774; *CWHC*, p. 499.

James Barnet Fry

1. Warner, Eicher, Spencer, and Fry's grave marker all list February 22, 1827, as Fry's date of birth. *GIB*, p. 162; *CWHC*, p. 246; *CWG*, pp. 82, 245. Welsh gives September 23, 1827, as the date of birth. *MHUG*, p. 120.

2. *GIB*, p. 162; *CWD*, p. 319; *CWHC*, p. 246.

3. *GIB*, p. 163; *MHUG*, p. 120; *CWD*, p. 319; *CWHC*, p. 246.

4. *GIB*, p. 163; *MHUG*, p. 121; *CWD*, p. 319; *CWHC*, p. 246.

John Grubb Parke

1. *GIB*, pp. 359-360; *CWD*, p. 618; *HTIE*, p. 556; *CWHC*, p. 416.

2. *GIB*, p. 360; *MHUG*, p. 251; *CWD*, p. 618; *HTIE*, p. 556; *CWHC*, p. 416.

3. *GIB*, p. 360; *MHUG*, p. 251; *CWD*, pp. 618-619; *HTIE*, p. 556; *CWHC*, p. 416.

4. *GIB*, p. 360; *MHUG*, p. 251; *CWD*, p. 619; *HTIE*, p. 556; *CWHC*, p. 416.

Isaac Jones Wistar

1. *GIB*, p. 568; *MHUG*, p. 373; *CWD*, p. 944; *CWHC*, p. 577; Wistar Institute, *Wistarabilia: A Centennial History of the Wistar Institute* (Philadelphia: The Wistar Institute, 1994), p. 5.

2. *GIB*, p. 568; *MHUG*, p. 374; *CWD*, p. 944; *CWHC*, p. 577; Wistar Institute, p. 5.

3. *GIB*, pp. 568-569; *MHUG*, pp. 374-375; *CWD*, p. 944; *CWHC*, p. 577.

4. *GIB*, p. 569; *MHUG*, pp. 375-376; *CWHC*, p. 577; Wistar Institute, pp. 5-6.

John Joseph Abercrombie

1. Abercrombie's precise date of birth is uncertain. Warner states that "upon the authority of a daughter, the date was March 4, 1798." *GIB*, p. 3. His grave marker shows March 28, 1798, as the date, although the word "July" was chiseled over the first part of the word "March." Welsh gives both March 4 and March 28 as the date of birth. *MHUG*, p. 1. Eicher and Spencer both give March 4, 1798, as the date. *CWHC*, p. 98; *CWG*, pp. 71, 220.

2. Warner, Welsh, Eicher, and Spencer all name Baltimore as the place of birth. *GIB*, p. 3; *MHUG*, p. 1; *CWHC*, p. 98; *CWG*, pp. 58, 220. Boatner gives Tennessee as the place of birth. *CWD*, p. 1. Warner states that "some sources record his birthplace as Tennessee." *GIB*, p. 3.

3. *GIB*, p. 3; *MHUG*, p. 1; *CWD*, p. 1; *CWHC*, p. 98.

4. *GIB*, p. 3; *MHUG*, p. 1; *CWD*, p. 1; *CWHC*, p. 98.

5. *GIB*, p. 3; *MHUG*, p. 1; *CWD*, pp. 1-2; *CWHC*, p. 98.

David Bell Birney

1. *GIB*, p. 34; *MHUG*, p. 29; *CWD*, p. 64; *HTIE*, p. 61; *GG*, p. 65; *CWHC*, p. 131.

2. *GIB*, p. 34; *MHUG*, p. 29; *CWD*, pp. 64-65; *HTIE*, p. 61; *GG*, pp. 65-67; *CWHC*, p. 132; *OR*, Series 1, vol. 11, pt. 1, p. 854.

3. *GIB*, pp. 34-35; *MHUG*, pp. 29-30; *CWD*, p. 65; *HTIE*, p. 61; *GG*, p. 67; *CWHC*, p. 132.

Alexander Hays

1. *GIB*, p. 223; *MHUG*, p. 164; *CWD*, p. 389; *HTIE*, p. 353; *GG*, p. 53; *CWHC*, p. 290.

2. *GIB*, pp. 223-224; *MHUG*, p. 164; *CWD*, p. 389; *HTIE*. pp. 353-354; *GG*, p. 53, *CWHC*, p. 290.

3. *GIB*, p. 224; *MHUG*, p. 164; *CWD*, pp. 389-390; *HTIE*, p. 354; *GG*, pp. 53-54; *CWHC*, p. 290.

Conrad Feger Jackson

1. *GIB*, pp. 246-247; *MHUG*, p. 181; *CWHC*, p. 315.

2. *GIB*, p. 247; *MHUG*, p. 181; *CWD*, p. 430; *CWHC*, p. 315.

3. *GIB*, p. 247; *MHUG*, p. 181; *CWD*, p. 430; *CWHC*, p. 315.

James Scott Negley

1. *GIB*, p. 341; *MHUG*, p. 239; *CWD*, p. 584; *CWHC*, p.404.

2. *GIB*, pp. 341-342; *CWD*, p. 584; *CWHC*, p. 404.

3. *GIB*, p. 342; *CWD*, p. 584; *CWHC*, p. 404; *OR*, Series 1, vol. 30, pt. 1, pp. 362-364, 1004-1053. The "Finding and Opinion in the Case of Major-General Negley" is found on pages 1043-1044.

4. *GIB*, p. 342; *CWD*, p, 584; *CWHC*, p. 404.

Thomas Algeo Rowley

1. Warner, Welsh, Eicher, and Spencer all give October 5, 1808, as Rowley's date of birth. *GIB*, p. 413; *MHUG*, p. 284; *CWHC*, p. 463; *CWG*, pp. 72, 282. Tagg states that Rowley was 55 as of the Battle of Gettysburg, which would make his birth year 1808. *GG*, p. 27. Boatner gives 1808 as Rowley's birth year. *CWD*, p. 711. Rowley's grave marker gives 1817 as the year of birth.

2. *GIB*, pp. 413-414; *MHUG*, p. 284; *CWD*, p. 711; *GG*, p. 27; *CWHC*, p. 463.

3. *GIB*, p. 414; *MHUG*, p. 284; *CWD*, p. 711; *GG*, pp. 27-28; *CWHC*, p. 463; *OR*, Series 1, vol. 11, pt. 1, p. 890.

4. *GIB*, p. 414; *MHUG*, p. 284; *CWD*, p. 711; *GG*, p. 28; *CWHC*, p. 463; *OR*, Series 1, vol. 29, pt. 2, p. 322.

5. *GIB*, p. 414; *MHUG*, p. 284; *CWD*, p. 711; *GG*, p. 28; *CWHC*, p. 463; *OR*, Series 1, vol. 40, pt. 2, p. 270; Lance J. Herdegen, "The Lieutenant Who Arrested A General," *The Gettysburg Magazine*, no. 4 (January 1991), pp.29-30.

6. Warner, Welsh, Eicher, and Spencer all give May 14, 1892, as Rowley's date of death. *GIB*, p. 414; *MHUG*, p. 284; *CWHC*, p. 463; *CWG*, pp. 185, 282. Boatner and Tagg state that Rowley died in 1892. *CWD*, p. 711; *GG*, p. 28. Rowley's grave marker gives 1893 as the year of death.

David Henry Williams

1. Warner reports that Williams' obituary in the Pittsburgh *Post*, June 2, 1891, stated that Williams took part in the Mexican War, but Warner also states that Williams does not appear in the traditional sources as an officer in that war. *GIB*, p. 561. Welsh and Eicher both state that Williams served in the Mexican War, but they do not provide any details as to the unit Williams served in or the time frame of his service in the war. *MHUG*, p. 370; *CWHC*, p. 615.

2. *GIB*, pp. 560-561; *MHUG*, p. 370; *CWHC*, p. 615.

3. *GIB*, p. 561; *MHUG*, p. 370; *CWD*, p. 927; *CWHC*, p. 615.

4. *GIB*, p. 561; *MHUG*, p. 370; *CWD*, p. 927; *CWHC*, p. 615.

5. *GIB*, p. 561; *MHUG*, p. 370; *CWD*, p. 927; *CWHC*, p. 615.

James Nagle

1. *GIB*, pp. 339-340; *MHUG*, p. 238; *CWD*, p. 238; *CWHC*, p. 403.

2. *GIB*, p. 340; *MHUG*, p. 238; *CWD*, p. 577; *CWHC*, p. 403.

3. *GIB*, p. 340; *MHUG*, pp. 238-239; *CWD*, pp. 577-578; *CWHC*, p. 403.

4. *GIB*, p. 340; *MHUG*, p. 239; *CWD*, p. 578; *CWHC*, p. 403.

David McMurtrie Gregg

1. *GIB*, pp. 187-188; *MHUG*, p. 140; *CWD*, p. 357; *HTIE*, p. 325; *GG*, p. 175; *CWHC*, p. 267; Milton V. Burgess, *David Gregg: Pennsylvania Cavalryman* (State College, PA: Nittany Valley Offset, 1984), pp. 1-31.

2. *GIB*, p. 188; *MHUG*, pp. 140-141; *CWD*, p. 357; *HTIE*, p. 325; *GG*, pp. 175-176; *CWHC*, p. 267; Burgess, pp. 32-92.

3. *GIB*, p. 188; *MHUG*, p. 141; *CWD*, p. 357; *HTIE*, p. 325; *CWHC*, p. 267; Burgess, pp. 93-106.

4. *GIB*, p. 188; *MHUG*, p. 141; *CWD*, p. 357; *HTIE*, p. 325; *GG*, p. 176; *CWHC*, p. 267; Burgess, pp. 107-113.

William High Keim

1. *GIB*, p. 259; *CWD*, p. 450; *CWHC*, p. 328.

2. *GIB*, pp. 259-260; *MHUG*, p. 189; *CWD*, p. 450; *CWHC*, p. 328.

3. *GIB*, p. 260; *MHUG*, 189; *CWD*, 450; *CWHC*, p. 328.

Alexander Schimmelfennig

1. *GIB*, pp. 423-424; *MHUG*, p. 289; *HTIE*, p. 661; *GG*, p. 138; *CWHC*, p. 472. Warner states that Schimmelfennig "served as an engineer officer in the Prussian army during the Schleswig-Holstein war and later in the revolution in Baden," but Warner has his facts mixed up regarding Schimmelfennig's involvement in these revolutionary causes. *GIB*, p. 423. As mentioned, Schimmelfennig's grave marker clearly states that he resigned from the Prussian Army and he supported the republican cause in the Schleswig-Holstein War and in Baden. This is why he fled to Switzerland and later emigrated to the United States. Welsh, Faust, Tagg, and Eicher correctly report Schimmelfennig's role in these matters.

2. *GIB*, p. 424; *MHUG*, p. 289; *CWD*, p. 725; *HTIE*, p. 661; *GG*, pp. 138-139; *CWHC*, p. 472.

3. *GIB*, p. 424; *MHUG*, p. 289; *CWD*, p. 725; *HTIE*, p. 661; *GG*, pp. 139-140; *CWHC*, p. 472.

4. *GIB*, p. 424; *MHUG*, pp. 289-290; *CWD*, p. 725; *HTIE*, p. 661; *CWG*, pp. 178, 283; *CWHC*, p. 472. Eicher gives September 7, 1865, as Schimmelfennig's date of death; however, Warner, Welsh, Faust, Spencer, and Schimmelfennig's grave marker all give September 5, 1865, as the date.

William Buel Franklin

1. *GIB*, p. 159; *MHUG*, p. 113; *CWD*, p. 303; *HTIE*, p. 285; *CWHC*, p. 243.

2. *GIB*, p. 159; *CWD*, pp. 303-304; *HTIE*, p. 285; *CWHC*, p. 243.

3. *GIB*, pp. 159-160; *MHUG*, p. 119; *CWD*, p. 304; *HTIE*, p. 285; *CWHC*, p. 243.

4. *GIB*, p. 160; *MHUG*, pp. 119-120; *CWD*, p. 304; *HTIE*, p. 285; *CWHC*, p. 243.

5. *GIB*, p. 160; *CWD*, p. 304; *HTIE*, p. 285; *CWHC*, p. 243.

BIBLIOGRAPHY

Ballard, Michael B. *Pemberton: A Biography*. Jackson, MS: University Press of Mississippi, 1991.

Blair, William Alan, editor. *A Politician Goes To War: The Civil War Letters of John White Geary*. University Park, PA: The Pennsylvania State University Press, 1995.

Boatner, Mark M. III. *The Civil War Dictionary*. New York: David McKay Company, Inc., 1959.

Burgess, Milton V. *David Gregg: Pennsylvania Cavalryman*. State College, PA: Nittany Valley Offset, 1984.

Cavanaugh, Michael A. "Introduction." In *Military Essays and Recollections of the Pennsylvania Commandery, Military Order of the Loyal Legion of the United States,* Vol. 1. Wilmington, NC: Broadfoot Publishing Company (Reprint), 1995.

Cleaves, Freeman. *Meade of Gettysburg*. Dayton, OH: Morningside Bookshop (Reprint), 1980.

Eicher, John H. and David J. Eicher. *Civil War High Commands*. Stanford, CA: Stanford University Press, 2001.

Faust, Patricia L., editor. *Historical Times Illustrated Encyclopedia of the Civil War*. New York: Harper & Row, 1986.

Herdegen, Lance J. "The Lieutenant Who Arrested A General," *The Gettysburg Magazine*, no. 4 (January 1991): 25-32.

Hennessy, John J. *Return to Bull Run: The Campaign and Battle of Second Manassas*. New York: Simon & Schuster, 1993.

Jordan, David M. *Winfield Scott Hancock: A Soldier's Life*. Bloomington, IN: Indiana University Press, 1988.

Lord, Francis A. *Lincoln's Railroad Man: Herman Haupt*. Rutherford, NJ: Fairleigh Dickinson University Press, 1969.

Magner, Blake A. *At Peace with Honor: The Civil War Burials of Laurel Hill Cemetery Philadelphia, Pennsylvania*. Collingswood, NJ: C.W. Historicals, 1997.

Nevins, James H. and William B. Styple. *What Death More Glorious: A Biography of General Strong Vincent*. Kearny, NJ: Belle Grove Publishing Co., 1997.

Nichols, Edward J. *Toward Gettysburg: A Biography of General John F. Reynolds.* University Park, PA: The Pennsylvania State University Press, 1958.

Spencer, James, compiler. *Civil War Generals: Categorical Listings and Biographical Directory.* New York: Greenwood Press, 1986.

Sully, Langdon. *No Tears For The General: The Life of Alfred Sully, 1821-1879.* Palo Alto, CA: American West Publishing Co., 1974.

Tagg, Larry. *The Generals of Gettysburg: The Leaders of America's Greatest Battle.* Campbell, CA: Savas Publishing Company, 1998.

Tucker, Glenn. *Hancock The Superb.* Dayton, OH: Morningside Bookshop (Reprint), 1980.

United States War Department, *The War of the Rebellion: A Compilation of the Official Records of the Union and Confederate Armies,* 70 vols. in 128 parts. Washington, D.C.: U.S. Government Printing Office, 1880-1901.

Ward, James A. *That Man Haupt: A Biography of Herman Haupt.* Baton Rouge, LA: Louisiana State University Press, 1973.

Warner, Ezra J. *Generals in Blue: Lives of the Union Commanders.* Baton Rouge, LA: Louisiana State University Press, 1964.

Warner, Ezra J. *Generals in Gray: Lives of the Confederate Commanders.* Baton Rouge, LA: Louisiana State University Press, 1959.

Welsh, Jack D. *Medical Histories of Confederate Generals.* Kent, OH: The Kent State University Press, 1995.

Welsh, Jack D. *Medical Histories of Union Generals.* Kent, OH: The Kent State University Press, 1996.

Wistar Institute. *Wistarabilia: A Centennial History of the Wistar Institute.* Philadelphia: The Wistar Institute, 1994.

ABOUT THE AUTHOR

DAVID L. CALLIHAN was born in Pittsburgh and raised in Charlotte, North Carolina. He received a BA in history from Duke University and graduated from the Dickinson School of Law in Carlisle, Pennsylvania. He is a life-long Civil War enthusiast and former licensed battlefield guide at Gettysburg National Military Park. After practicing law for 19 years in Pennsylvania, David decided to devote his full time to studying and writing about the war. He has had five articles published in *The Gettysburg Magazine* and he is the editor/publisher of *Grave Matters* (www.gravematters.net), which is a newsletter about Civil War grave sites. David resides in Dryden, New York, with his wife, Jean.

3-31-06

DATE DUE			